THEOCRITUS

BION

MOSCHUS

T0371204

THEOCRITUS

BION AND MOSCHUS

TRANSLATED INTO ENGLISH VERSE

BY

ARTHUR S. WAY, D.Lit.

AUTHOR OF TRANSLATIONS INTO ENGLISH VERSE OF HOMER'S ILIAD AND ODYSSEY,
OF AESCHYLUS, SOPHOCLES AND EURIPIDES,
THE GEORGICS OF VIRGIL, ETC.

Cambridge :

at the University Press

1913

CAMBRIDGE
UNIVERSITY PRESS

University Printing House, Cambridge CB2 8BS, United Kingdom

Published in the United States of America by Cambridge University Press, New York

Cambridge University Press is part of the University of Cambridge.

It furthers the University's mission by disseminating knowledge in the pursuit of
education, learning and research at the highest international levels of excellence.

www.cambridge.org
Information on this title: www.cambridge.org/9781107696730

© Cambridge University Press 1913

This publication is in copyright. Subject to statutory exception
and to the provisions of relevant collective licensing agreements,
no reproduction of any part may take place without the written
permission of Cambridge University Press.

First published 1913
First paperback edition 2014

A catalogue record for this publication is available from the British Library

ISBN 978-1-107-69673-0 Paperback

Cambridge University Press has no responsibility for the persistence or accuracy of
URLs for external or third-party internet websites referred to in this publication,
and does not guarantee that any content on such websites is, or will remain, accurate
or appropriate.

INTRODUCTION

WHEN we have said that Theocritus "flourished" about the middle of the third century B.C., that he was a native of Sicily, that he knew Southern Italy, the Isles of Greece, and Alexandria, we have practically got to the end of the external evidence respecting him, though much may be gathered, and much more inferred, from the internal evidence of his poems.

Of Bion and Moschus we know no more than that the former, whose date is unknown, was a native of Asia Minor, that the latter was a Sicilian, and "flourished" about the middle of the second century B.C.

I have not held it to be part of a translator's office to discuss, far less to decide, whether all the poems traditionally ascribed to Theocritus were really composed by him, or whether half of them must be awarded to some nebulous Bacon of his own or a later period. I tacitly plead on his behalf the possession which, even in literary property, should be nine points of the law.

A. S. W.

March, 1913.

CONTENTS

THE IDYLLS OF THEOCRITUS.

IDYLL I.

A talk between a goat-herd and a shepherd leads up to the " Song of Daphnis." Daphnis had vowed eternal constancy to his first love, a Nymph ; whereupon Aphrodite made him love a strange maiden ; but, sooner than break his vow, he let this passion waste him to his death.

THYRSIS.

SWEET is the whispering, friend goat-herd, of yonder pine
Low-lisping its song by the spring, and sweet that piping of thine.
Pan's is the peerless voice ; thou art second to him alone.
If the horned he-goat be his choice, by thee is the she-goat won :
If the prize of the Forest-lord be the she-goat, thy song's wage
Is a kid, and sweet on the board is her flesh, till the milking-age.

GOAT-HERD.

Nay, shepherd, 'tis thou art the wonder : more sweet is the sound of
    thy singing
Than the echoing laughter yonder of the stream from the cliff's brow
    springing.
If the Queens of Song Divine bear off the ewe for their prize,   [10
Yet the stall-fed lamb shall be thine : but and if it be good in their eyes
With the guerdon-lamb to content them, the ewe thy song shall crown.

THYRSIS.

For the Nymphs' sake, goat-herd, consent even here to sit thee down,
Here, where the slant-sloped knoll and the tamarisks wait for thee,
And to waken the wood-pipe's soul. Thy goats shall be tended of me.

B

GOAT-HERD.

O shepherd, I dare not in heat of the noontide, I dare not raise
The strain ; for I fear to meet great Pan in his wrath : from the chase
Forwearied then, doth he lay him down to his rest, and grim
Is the wrath that is ambushed aye by the quivering nostrils of him.
Nay then—for Daphnis' pain hath been sung, O Thyrsis, of thee,   [20
And the Mount of the Pastoral Strain hast thou higher ascended than we—
Hither, and let us recline beneath yon elm, that shades
The front of the Garden-god's shrine, and the cell of the Fountain-maids,
Where the shepherds' seats curve round 'neath the oaks.   If thou wilt
        sing now
As when Chromis of Libya found what a lord of song wast thou,
Thrice shalt thou with my good will milk the mother of twins, my pride :
Two pails will the milk of her fill when her kids have been satisfied.
    And an ivy-wood bowl shalt thou gain, with sweet wax varnished fair,
New-carven, with handles twain, and the scent of the scoop still there.
And around its lips go twining the ivy-leaves crowning the rim :
Star-dust of the helichryse gleameth thereon, and a tendril seemeth   30
To exult in its golden-shining berries that girdle the brim.
And within is a maiden—she might have been carved by a God's own
        hand—
In mantle and coif fair-dight ; and beside her lovers stand,
Two young men beautiful-tressed, and they fling from side to side
Each at other the gibe and the jest ; but untouched doth her heart abide ;
But a look now laughter-dancing she flasheth on one of the twain ;
At the other anon is she glancing : they pine in love's long pain
With pale tired eyes ; but their toil and their sighs are spent in vain.
    And thereby is a fisher, an old man ; crouched on a rock is he :
For a cast he upgathers the fold of a great net eagerly ;   40
And the grey-haired seemeth as one that toileth with might and main :
Thou wouldst say that his fishing was done with his strong limbs' utter-
        most strain.
So stand out down the length of his neck the sinews : in sooth,
Grey-haired though he be, his strength is even as the strength of youth.

And withdrawn from the sea-worn sire but a little space is a garth
Whose lovely vines by the fire-red clusters are bowed to the earth ;
And a little lad on the height of the stone dyke warding them sits :
Two foxes to left and to right of him prowl : one stealthily flits
Through the vine-rows devouring the grapes, while the other a guileful
    plot
For the boy's food-wallet shapes, and she vows she will leave him not 50
Until she may flee thence leaving him stranded, of breakfast bare :
But a locust-trap is he weaving of asphodel-stalks wrought fair,
And with rushes he intertwines it : his scrip no whit he minds,
Neither the plundered vines, such joy in his plaiting he finds.
    And the rippling acanthus embracing floats all round the bowl,
A marvel of delicate chasing ; it would strike with amaze thy soul.
A goat for its price I paid to a sailor from Calydon,
And a great cream-cheese I laid in his hands ere the prize was won.
Not once have I lifted it up to my lips, but unsullied it stands
Still. That selfsame cup will I gladly give to thine hands   60
If thou sing that heart-thrilling song, O friend, for the which I long :
I begrudge it no whit. Ah come, dear friend ! Thou canst not keep
Thy song in the Unseen Home, in the all-forgetting sleep.

THYRSIS.

    Wake, O sweet Song-queens, yea, now wake ye the Herdman's Lay.
Thyrsis of Etna is this, and the voice of his singing it is.
Where were ye, Nymphs, in the hour when Daphnis pined to his
    dying ?—
Where the crests of Pindus tower ?—in Peneius' dells fair-lying ?
For not by Anapus the bright broad flood were ye wandering,
Nor on Etna's watchtower-height, nor by Acis' hallowed spring.
    Wake, O sweet Song-queens, yea, now wake ye the Herdman's Lay.   70
For him was the lynxes' moan, and the wolves' long howl for him,
And the lion's thunderous groan for the dead thrilled oakwoods dim.
    Wake, O sweet Song-queens, yea, now wake ye the Herdman's Lay.
Couched at his feet ere he died, mourned kine and bulls enow,
Heifers for sorrow that sighed, and young calves moaning low.

Wake, O sweet Song-queens, yea, now wake ye the Herdman's Lay.
From the mountain did Hermes come the first, and " Daphnis," he spake,
" Whom lovest thou so ?   For whom doth thine heart with anguish
    break ? "
Wake, O sweet Song-queens, yea, now wake ye the Herdman's Lay.
Thronged neat-herds and shepherds around, came goat-herds gather-
    ing,   80
All questioning touching his wound ; came thither the Garden-king
Crying, " Daphnis, why pine with love ?   I know a maiden fair
Who seeks thee by fountain and grove, whose feet flit everywhere—
Wake, O sweet Song-queens, yea, now wake ye the Herdman's Lay—
In the quest. O a laggard art thou in love, and a feeble-wit !
Men have called thee a neat-herd—I trow, 'tis for herding of goats thou
    art fit !
For the goat-herd, whene'er he espies his goats at their amorous play,
Gazeth with yearning eyes, and would fain be even as they :—
Wake, O sweet Song-queens, yea, now wake ye the Herdman's Lay—
Thou seest the maiden-throng, and thou hearest their laughter ring-
    ing,   90
And with languishing eyes dost thou long with these in the dance to be
    swinging."
Yet never a word he replied, but set him to dree the weird
Of his bitter love, and abide the doom whose goal he neared.
Wake, O sweet Song-queens, yea, now wake ye the Herdman's Lay.
And the Queen of Love drew nigh, with her subtle inscrutable smile—
But still did the stern wrath lie hidden under her lips' sweet guile.
" Ha, Daphnis, and thou didst say," she whispered, " that thou wouldst
    throw
Love !—hath not a stronger this day laid that proud boaster low ? "
Wake, O sweet Song-queens, yea, now wake ye the Herdman's Lay.
" Tyrannous Cypris ! "—keen scorn rang in the answering word   100
Of Daphnis—" rancorous Queen, O Cypris by mortals abhorred !
All things are proclaiming, I ween, that the sun of my life hath set ;
Yet even from the Land Unseen will I deal to thy Love wounds
    yet ! "

Wake, O sweet Song-queens, yea, now wake ye the Herdman's Lay.
Yea, there is it told how he cried unto Cypris, " To Ida go !
To thy minion Anchises speed, by the oak and the sighing reed !
But peacefully bees beside the hives here murmur low.
   Wake, O sweet Song-queens, yea, now wake ye the Herdman's Lay.
Thine Adonis is young, is fair, and the flock doth he feed and fold,
And he smiteth the trembling hare, and he chaseth the beasts of the
    wold.   110
   Wake, O sweet Song-queens, yea, now wake ye the Herdman's Lay.
Draw nigh Diomedes again, and dare him to face thy might !
Cry, ' Daphnis the herd have I slain : now meet me thou in fight ! '
   Wake, O sweet Song-queens, yea, now wake ye the Herdman's Lay.
Wolves, lynxes, and bears that drowse through the winter in caves of
    the glen,
Farewell ! Your Daphnis shall rouse not the forest-echoes again !
Woods, glades, ye shall see him no more : Arethusa, many farewells !
Farewell, ye rivers that pour bright streams down Thymbris' dells !
   Wake, O sweet Song-queens, yea, now wake ye the Herdman's Lay.
That selfsame Daphnis am I who pastured the kine in the mead,   120
And the bulls to the springs hereby and the calves I wont to lead.
   Wake, O sweet Song-queens, yea, now wake ye the Herdman's Lay.
Pan, Pan, from the long crag-towers of Lycaeus, if there thou be,
Or where Maenalus' huge cliff towers art roaming, to Sicily
From Helicas' barrow O come ! Let Lycaon's son for a space
Lie lone in the high-reared tomb whereon Gods marvelling gaze.
   Come away, Song-queens, refrain : hush, hush ye the Herdfolk's strain !
Come, take from mine hand this sweet-breathed pipe, O Forest-king,
Fair-moulded with wax : to meet thy lip doth it curve and cling.
Dragged downward by Love are my feet unto Hades, where no pipes
    ring.   130
   Come away, Song-queens, refrain : hush, hush ye the Herdfolk's strain !
Now let thorns be with violets o'erspread ; bear pansies, ye thistles, now !
Let the lovely narcissus shed its curls o'er the juniper-bough.
Be turmoil and change everywhere ; let the pine's arms bend with the
    pear ;

For Daphnis is dying, is dying! The hounds let the stag pull down:
Let owls from the hills replying the chant of the nightingale drown!"
    Come away, Song-queens, refrain: hush, hush ye the Herdfolk's strain!
He spake, and his voice was stilled. Aphrodite repented o'erlate,
And had raised up him she had killed—but all the threads of his fate
Had by this run out, and along death's flood was Daphnis swept, 140
The man by the Queens of Song beloved, and for whom Nymphs wept.
    Come away, Song-queens, refrain: hush, hush ye the Herdfolk's strain!
Now give thou the bowl and the goat: of her milk an offering
To the Queens of Song will I pour. Farewell to you o'er and o'er,
Song-queens, and a sweeter note ere long unto you will I sing.

GOAT-HERD.

May thy lips for thy song divine, O Thyrsis, with honey be filled,
And with honeycombs drop, and the sweet dried Aegilan grape mayst
    thou eat!
For notes clear-ringing as thine hath never cicala shrilled.
Lo, here is the cup: mark thou what odours around it cling:
Thou wouldst say it was dipped but now in the Hours' rose-scented
    spring.   150
Kissaitha, draw near! Thou art free to milk her. She-goats, have a
    care
That ye skip not frolicsomely: of the he-goat's onrush beware!

IDYLL II.

The girl Simaetha, forsaken by her lover Delphis, essays to win him back by magical spells and incantations. As she burns her charms, she turns a brazen wheel.

WHERE are the bay-leaves ? Where are the love-syrups ? Thestylis, bring
These hither : the bowl set there, and with crimson wool enring.
For against yon rebel lover twined shall the witch-knots be,
Seeing twelve days now have passed over since his feet drew nigh unto me,
He knows not if we have died, or if yet living we are :
Not once his buffet hath tried my door, but away and afar
Aphrodite and Eros fly me, and his fickle soul have they borne.
To the wrestling-ring will I hie me of Timagetus to-morn
To see him : for his false dealing with me will I chide him there :
But now with enchantments sealing him mine will I work.   Shine fair, 10
O Moon, for the Song of the Spell unto thee shall be softly chanted,
And to Hecate Queen of Hell : the very dogs cower, daunted,
As o'er corpses and mounds of the dead, and o'er dark-clotted blood she
    doth wend.
Hail to thee, Hecate dread ! Stand by me thou to the end,
Fashioning charms outdone by naught that Circe prepared,
Or Medea, or that weird one, Perimede the golden-haired.
   Draw, magic Wheel of Power, yon truant to love to my bower.
Lo, first must smoulder the grain on the fire : haste, straw it thereon,
Thestylis—out, scatterbrain ! whither now be thy senses gone ?   [20
How, in thine eyes am I vile ?—dost thou mock at my love-lorn moans ?
Straw it, and murmur the while : " I am strewing Delphis' bones."
   Draw, magic Wheel of Power, yon truant to love to my bower.
Delphis hath done to me shame and wrong, and the bay burn I
Over Delphis.   Touched by the flame like a living thing doth it cry !

Suddenly is it consumed, till we see not an ash-fleck grey :—
May the flesh of Delphis the doomed in fire so waste away !
Draw, magic Wheel of Power, yon truant to love to my bower.
As I melt in the fire's red glow this wax, with the Goddess to aid me,
May love melt Delphis so, that Myndian who betrayed me ;
And, as turns this brazen plate, whirled round by my fingers, so   30
By the Love-queen's spell at my gate may he restlessly turn to and fro !
Draw, magic Wheel of Power, yon truant to love to my bower.
Now burn I the husks ; and thou, O Artemis, bow to my will
Hell's ruthless Lord—yea, bow whatsoever is stubborner still !
Hark, Thestylis ! ringeth the street with the baying of dogs in their fear !
The Goddess where three ways meet—the castanets, clash them !—is near.
Draw, magic Wheel of Power, yon truant to love to my bower.
Lo, hushed is the face of the sea, the breezes are hushed to rest :
But mine heart's fierce agony is hushed not within my breast ;
But for him is my soul aflame who made me—alas the day !—   40
No wife, but a thing of shame, a maiden no more for aye.
Draw, magic Wheel of Power, yon truant to love to my bower.
Thrice from the bowl I spill the drops, O Queen, thrice crying :
" Be it woman or minion that still in those false arms is lying,
May their memory out of his breast fleet wholly, as Theseus of yore
Forgat the lovely-tressed Ariadne on Dia's shore."
Draw, magic Wheel of Power, yon truant to love to my bower.
A plant to Arcadian men is known ; nor foal nor steed
Nor mare, mid mountain and glen, but is mad for the coltsfoot weed :
Even Delphis thus may I see ; from the glistening wrestling-ring   50
As one possessed may he flee, to my dwelling hastening.
Draw, magic Wheel of Power, yon truant to love to my bower.
This fringe but a short while past did Delphis from his attire
Lose : now do I shred it, and cast the threads on the red fierce fire.
Ah, torturing love, why then hast thou fastened on me, to drain,
Close-clinging as leech of the fen, my blood from every vein ?
Draw, magic Wheel of Power, yon truant to love to my bower.
To-morn will I pound me an eft, and an evil drink shall be here.
But the magic herbs that be left now, Thestylis, take thou, and smear

Their juice on his lintel—mine own heart lies chained down on its
    stone, 60
Even as I say it ; but none account doth he take of my moans ;—
And murmur, spitting thereon : " I am smearing Delphis' bones."
    Draw, magic Wheel of Power, yon truant to love to my bower.
Alone am I now, to bewail the curse that hath come with my love.
How shall I begin the tale ?   Who made me partaker thereof ?
Anaxo the maund-bearer sought me one day, and would fain have brought
    me
Unto Artemis' precinct, where wild beasts in procession were led
In the Goddess's honour, and there in their midst was a lioness dread.
    Think on me, Moon, as I tell of my love, and how it befell. [70
And Theucaridas' servant from Thrace, the nurse—now laid in the tomb—
Which dwelt near neighbour to me, besought me earnestly
On that pomp of procession to gaze ; and I, drawn on by my doom,
In linen white low-trailing forth of my chamber I passed :
Clearista's mantle o'erveiling my shoulders about me I cast.
    Think on me, Moon, as I tell of my love, and how it befell.
In the midst of the highway we were by this, by Lycaon's abode—
Lo, Delphis beheld I there, and his friend, as onward they strode.
More golden than flowered helichryse their cheeks' bloom showed to mine
    eyes :
Far whiter, O Moon, than thou gleamed out the breasts of the twain
Who were newly come but now from the graceful athlete-strain. 80
    Think on me, Moon, as I tell of my love, and how it befell.
When I saw him, when madness caught me, pierced was my soul with
    pain ;
All beauty was stricken with blight, and for all that goodly sight
Naught cared I : of this knew I naught, how I came to mine home again
Thence ; but through all my frame a sudden fever burned.
Ten days on a bed of flame, ten nights, I tossed and turned.
    Think on me, Moon, as I tell of my love, and how it befell.
Even as the boxwood, paling ever, my hue had grown ;
Mine hair from mine head was failing, nothing but skin and bone
Was left of me, worn and weak.   Whereunto did I not seek ? 90

Unto what grey chanter of strains love-binding had I not gone ?
But relief came none to my pains, and the time went fleeting on.
  Think on me, Moon, as I tell of my love, and how it befell.
To mine handmaid I opened my mind at the last, and the truth I
    told :
" Up, Thestylis, now must thou find a salve for the stricken-souled ;
For possessed am I, body and heart, by the Myndian.   Up, then, depart,
And thou by the wrestling-ground of Timagetus be my spy ;
For there is he chiefly found, and he loveth to sit thereby.
  Think on me, Moon, as I tell of my love, and how it befell.
Watch till alone he shall be, then sign to him secretly ;   100
Say ' Simaetha calleth for thee,' and privily lead him to me."
I spake, and she went, and anon came bringing that radiant one,
Delphis, to mine abode : as with wings in his feet he passed
My threshold-stone, and he trode my floor at last—at last !
  Think on me, Moon, as I tell of my love, and how it befell.
Then chill mine heart's blood grew as the snow ; from my brow in that
    hour,
Heavy-dropping as summer-night dew, did the dew of my passion pour.
Not a word, not a word could I speak, not so much as the faint low cry
Of a babe in a dream of fear, which only the mother can hear.
As a carven image, weak and numbed did my fair form lie.   110
  Think on me, Moon, as I tell of my love, and how it befell.
Under eyelashes earthward-drooping one glance he flashed upon me—
O loveless one !—and stooping to my bed low murmured he :
" Thy bidding to this dear door, and my coming to seek thy face—
One ran, O Simaetha, before the other by no more space
Than was gained by my feet when Philinus the fleet was outstripped in
    the race :
  Think on me, Moon, as I tell of my love, and how it befell.
For myself was at point to come—by sweet Love swear I to thee—
Even this night, to thine home, with friends or twain or three,
With the Wine-god's quinces golden in the breast of my tunic enfolden,120
And a silver-poplar wreath, even Herakles' sacred bough,
With purple bands beneath and above twined, set on my brow.

Think on me, Moon, as I tell of my love, and how it befell.
And if ye had welcomed me in, my friends had rejoiced with me then,
For the crown of beauty I win and of swiftness mid all young men :
Content had I been to press on thy lips of loveliness
One kiss.   But and if ye had driven me thence from the doors barred fast,
With torch and with axe had we riven a breach wherethrough we had
    passed.
Think on me, Moon, as I tell of my love, and how it befell.
And now are my thanks, I ween, due first to the Cyprian Queen,   130
And, next to the Cyprian, to thee, who hast plucked me forth of the fire,
Sweet, bidding me unto thee, unto Love's own Bower of Desire,
Love-scorched as I am : oft Love lights fierier flames in the breast
Than the Fire-god kindled above red Lipara's burning crest.
Think on me, Moon, as I tell of my love, and how it befell.
By his madness dread doth he chase from her bower the maid, and the
    bride
From the bridal couch, from her place yet warm by her own lord's side."
    Then I—O easy to woo was I !—when thus he had said,
Laid hold on his hand, and drew him down on mine own soft bed.
Then heart into heart beat fire ; then, then did our faces meet   140
Hot with our fervent desire, and we murmured things most sweet.
Why linger long on the tale, dear Moon, now all is in vain !—
Mighty is Love to prevail, and his pleasure was wrought of twain.
No fault did we find in each other, there breathed no word of blame
Till yesterday : ah, but the mother of Philista the flute-player came
To-day, when the steeds immortal from Ocean endless-flowing
Bore up to the heavenly portal Dawn of the arms rose-glowing ;
And, with divers nothings, she told me how Delphis' love hath strayed,
That a minion doth captive hold him, or haply a rival maid.   [150
Naught certainly could she declare, save this, that he brimmed evermore
The cup to an absent fair, and at last fled forth of the door,
Crying, " I'll wreathe yon dwelling with garlands bright of hue ! "
This was the tale of her telling—and oh, it is true, it is true !
For thrice, four times unto me would he come 'twixt morn and eve,
And his oil-cruse trustfully in my keeping he wont to leave.

But in vain have I watched for him, lonely through twelve days' weary
    tide—
Can it be he forgetteth me only, that he loveth none beside ?
I will bind him with love-spells now : but and if he shall turn into hate
My love, by the Fates I vow, he shall knock at Hades' gate !
Such drugs, a deadly store, in a casket lie to mine hand :   160
I won, Queen, this dark lore from a woman of Morning-land.
    Farewell, Queen ; turn thy rein, let thy steeds into Ocean descend.
I will bear my burden of pain, as I have borne, unto the end.
O Moon of the radiant face, farewell ! Farewell to your light,
O stars that for ever race by the wheels of quiet Night !

IDYLL III.

A goat-herd's serenade to his love, who lives, like a Wood-nymph, in a cave.

UNTO Amaryllis' dwelling, singing my love, have I wended :
My goats on the hill green-swelling are grazing, by Tityrus tended.
O best-loved Tityrus, feed my goats with diligent heed !
To the well-spring guide them down ; but, Tityrus, still have a care
Of the Libyan he-goat brown, lest he butt thee unaware.

  Oh Amaryllis my sweet, why through this cavern dost thou
Never flash one glance to greet thy lover ?—dost hate me now ?
Ah, dost thou account me foul of feature, now we have met ?—
With the nose of an ape, or the jowl of a boar ?—I shall hang myself
    yet !
Lo, apples ten have I brought thee : I gathered the honey-hued store 10
Where thou badest that they should be sought, and to-morn will I bring
    yet more.
Ah, look on mine anguish, how burns my wound !—oh, would I might win
The wings of a murmuring bee, to enter thy cavern to thee,
To slip through the ivy and ferns whose green veil closes thee in !
Love—tyrannous god ! too well do I know him : a lioness grim
Gave him suck ; and his dam in a dell of the wild-wood cradled him.
His fire bites deep to the bone, doth creep round every limb.
Ebon-browed girl ! love-glancing eyes ! O heart of stone !
Let thine arms close round me, my sweet ! let thy lips and my lips
    meet !—
For oh, there is bliss entrancing in barren kisses alone.   20
Soon, soon wilt thou drive me to tearing in pieces small this wreath,
Amaryllis, my dear, my dear, that for thee I am treasuring here,

With rosebuds twined for thy wearing, and with parsley of odorous
  breath !
  Woe's me, the forlorn one !—and wilt thou not hearken ?—what fate
  shall be mine ?
I will fling from me this skin kilt, I will leap mid the rolling brine
Where fisherman Olpis doth keep keen watch till the tunnies ap-
  pear :
Yea, if to my death I leap, with joy of my death wilt thou hear !
I knew, when I sought to divine if thou lovest me—knew my doom ;
For the orpine-leaf, when I smote, gave back no answering note,
But withered, with never a sign, on my arm lay the petal-bloom.   30
Agroio, who turneth the sieves for divining, cruelly
Spake truth, as she bound the sheaves of harvest, that I of thee
Into thraldom am brought, soul and body ; but naught thou carest
  for me.
A she-goat for thee am I warding, a snow-white mother of twain :
But Erithakis begs for the prize, that gipsy of soft dark eyes—
And shall win it, for thy disregarding of me, thou Queen of Dis-
  dain !
  My right eye quivered and shook !—O love, thy face shall I see ?
I will sing, the while I recline against yon whispering pine ;
And perchance upon me will she look ; not adamant wholly is she.
              (*Sings " The Lay of the Lovers of Old."*)
" Hippomenes, fain to wed with the storm-footed maiden, brought   40
Apples in hand as he sped in the race : Atalanta caught
One glimpse—down deep in love's sea did she leap with heart dis-
  traught.
Melampus the seer led down unto Pylos from Othrys the kine
Whereby that bride of renown, O Bias, was won to be thine ;
And Alphesiboea, a crown of wisdom, she bare to thy line.
For Adonis, the shepherd who pastured his flock 'neath the green hill-
  crest,
Cytherea was love-overmastered : such madness thrilled her breast,
That, by death unremoved, still her dead, her beloved, to her bosom is
  pressed.

But oh for the stirless sleep on Endymion cast by the kiss
Of Selene !   O might I reap, sweet girl, Iasion's bliss   50
In rapture to strain[1]—but for ears profane no tale is this."

My throbbing temples beat—thou car'st not !   My song is done :
I will cast me down, to be meat for the wolves to banquet upon :—
But as honey will this be sweet to thy lips, O cruel one !

1. Iasion won the love of the goddess Demeter.

IDYLL IV.

The goat-herd Battus finds his friend Corydon acting as neat-herd to the athlete Aegon, who has gone to compete at the Olympic Games.

BATTUS.

TELL, Corydon, whose may they be, these kine ?   Is Philondas their lord ?

CORYDON.

Nay, Aegon : he gave them to me, in the meadow to feed them and ward.

BATTUS.

And at even thou still goest halves in the milk of them all, I ween.

CORYDON.

Nay, his old sire putteth the calves to the dams—O, his eyes are keen !

BATTUS.

But the master—where doth he flee us ?   Whither from sight hath he
    sped ?

CORYDON.

Hast heard not ?—away to Alphoeus our champion hath Milo led.

BATTUS.

Him ?—when did the eyes of him light on the oil of the wrestlers' play ?

CORYDON.

Against Herakles' self could his might be matched in contest—they say.

BATTUS.

Ay, so did my mother declare that Pollux by me was outdone !

CORYDON.

So is it : a spade doth he bear, and a score of his sheep :[1] he is gone.   10

BATTUS.

This Milo will lesson, I trow, the wolves ere long to rage !

CORYDON.

For their lord do the heifers low, and pine at their pasturage.

BATTUS.

Hapless are these, I vow, such a pitiful master is theirs !

CORYDON.

Hapless indeed : yea, now not one for the pasture cares.

BATTUS.

See there : to a frame all bone doth the hide of yon heifer cling !
Doth she feed upon dewdrops alone, like the grigs through the grass that
    spring ?

CORYDON.

Nay, nay ; but whiles do I lead her where Aesarus' waters flow,
And armfuls of grass of the mead, soft fodder, before her I throw ;
And whiles in the shade of Latymnius' glade doth she skip to and fro.

BATTUS.

And yon red bull, how thin !—may such an one fall one day   20
Unto Lamprias' sons to win, when sacrifice-dues they pay
Unto Hera : for still devisers of ill in their hearts be they.

CORYDON.

And yet to the river-mead is he driven, where Physcus doth flow,
And anon to Neaethus, to feed where all things beautiful grow ;
And to odorous beeswort I lead him, where endive and goatwort blow.

   1. Digging exercise was part of the prescribed training for athletes : their appetite
was proverbially enormous.

BATTUS.

Alack! thy kine will go down unto Hades, 'tis all too plain,
Poor Aegon, since thou for renown of triumph accursèd art fain!
And the pipe that of old thou didst fashion doth mould befleck and stain.

CORYDON.

That pipe?—by the Nymphs, not so! He gave me the dainty thing
When to Pisa he passed; and, I trow, I too can skill to sing: 30
I can chant the Glauce-lays, I can warble the Pyrrhus-ditty,
Crotona the fair can I praise, and Zacynthus the goodly city,
And Lacinium dayspring-bright, where our boxer of matchless might,
This Aegon, devoured with ease broad barley-cakes three-score.
There too by the hoofs did he seize that bull, and downward bore
From the mountain, his small keepsake for his Amaryllis: the throng
Of her handmaids screamed; but he brake into laughter loud and long.

BATTUS.

Alas, Amaryllis the fair!—thou art dead, but I cannot forget thee,
Lost love, mine heart's one star! Not dearer my she-goats are!
Woe's me for my doom of despair, for the cruel fate that met thee!   40

CORYDON.

Take heart, friend Battus: thy night may end in a fairer day:
The living may yet hope on: hopeless the dead are alone.
Sometimes doth the heaven wax bright, it raineth not alway.

BATTUS.

I endure—ah, pelt from the brow yon calves!—at the olive-sprays there
The rogues are nibbling now!

CORYDON.

Shoo, Silver-coat, out!—you dare!—
Flame-coat, will you not heed?—shoo! hence to the slope of the hill!
A bad end will I deal you!—indeed, by the Forest-king, but I will,
If you get not away hence!—quick!—why, back again is she stealing!
O for my hare-hunting stick! I would try if your hide hath feeling!

BATTUS.

For heaven's sake, Corydon, see—'neath mine ankle the spike of a
    thistle   [50
This moment hath pierced! O me, how densely here do they bristle,
The arrow-head thorns! May a bad end come to thine heifer! The
    sting
As I gaped at her, pierced me. My lad, prithee say dost thou see the
    thing?

CORYDON.

Yes, yes: and my nails have laid hold now—behold the same!

BATTUS.

How tiny a wound has it made!—yet how tall a man can it lame!

CORYDON.

When next to the mountain you go, friend Battus, go not unshod,
For thorns and briers grow there; rough are the paths to be trod.

BATTUS.

Doth our greybeard clip and kiss—good Corydon, prithee say—
That black-browed sweeting of his, who enthralled him once on a day?

CORYDON.

Ay, now as ever. I came on them both beside the byre   60
But lately: still doth he flame with the heat of the olden fire.

BATTUS.

Well done, Master Frisk! of thy blood art thou verily near of kin
To the Satyrs, or sons of the wood, Pan's children goatish of shin!

IDYLL V.

A quarrel between a goat-herd and a shepherd, ending in a contest in song.

COMATAS.

My she-goats, keep ye away from yon shepherd, Sibyrtas' slave,
Yon Lacon : but yesterday he stole my goatskin, the knave !

LACON.

Away from the green well-side ! Do ye mark not the evil soul,
My lambs ? At dawning-tide my pipe Comatas stole.

COMATAS.

What pipe ?—O Sibyrtas' slave, and prithee, when hadst thou one ?
And doth it suffice not thee upon cracked straws two or three
To squeal a pitiful stave beside thy Corydon ?

LACON.

'Twas a present, and Lycon the giver, Sir Freeman—but pray what skin
From thee was filched away by Lacon ?—Comatas, say !
Why, Eumaras thy lord had never such thing, to sleep therein !   10

COMATAS.

That dappled one Crocylus gave, what time to the Nymphs he had slain
A she-goat. O thou knave, thou didst pine with envy to gain
My prize : and at last to thy clutch hath it passed—and bare I remain !

LACON.

By the Shore-king Pan do I swear, never Lacon, Calaethis' child,
Of thy skin-coat stripped thee bare ; else may I, in madness wild,
From the sheer crags hurl me, there above swift Crathis piled !

COMATAS.

By the Nymphs of the Mere, whose shrine stands yonder, I swear unto
 thee,
Good fellow—so be they benign and gracious still unto me !—
Never stolen was pipe of thine by Comatas privily.

LACON.

If thy word or thine oath I take, may I suffer all Daphnis' woe !   20
But a kid, if thou wilt, do thou stake—it is not for mine honour, I
 know—
Against thee will I sing till thou yield, till I bring thine arrogance low.

COMATAS.

" Athena was challenged once to a singing-match by a sow ! "
Lo, staked is my kid : come, dunce, thy fatted lamb stake thou.

LACON.

Ha, fox !—and this were a fair stake, quotha, betwixt us two !
Who ever would card coarse hair when he might comb wool ?—and
 who,
When a young milch-goat stood there, his milk from a foul bitch
 drew ?

COMATAS.

That doth he who looks to o'ercome his betters in singing, like thee :—
" A wasp with his droning hum would meet the cicala ! " But, see,
My kid is no stake—for a he-goat's sake, then, sing against me.   30

LACON.

Not so fast !—not afire is thine house !—thou wilt sing far more at
 thine ease
'Neath yon wild olive's boughs, and under the shade of the trees ;
For a cool stream there is flowing ; thick groweth the grass thereby ;
There's a bed of the wildwood's strowing, and the locust's musical cry.

COMATAS.

Not I am in haste ; but much do I chafe that thou art so bold
That thine eyes, with never a touch of shame, look at me, who of old
Taught a boy, the ingrate here—of his gratitude this is the end !
" Wolf-cubs mid thy dogs do thou rear—they will turn upon thee and
    will rend."

LACON.

And when from thee did I hear, did I learn, aught worthy to win
For a treasure of memory—mere ape, jealous mannikin ?   40

COMATAS.

When I gave thee the stick, such a beating, thy screams from the she-
    goats round
Wakened a chorus of bleating ; the he-goat danced to the sound.

LACON.

Hunchback, take heed lest I lay thee yet lower, ay, in thy grave !
Come on ! to the strife away !—thou shalt sing thy latest stave !

COMATAS.

Not thither I go ! hereby grows galingale, spread oak-trees,
Here sweetly and dreamily by the hives hum murmuring bees ;
There be cool-welling fountains twain : here babbles the birds' wild
    strain
From trees : this arbour of mine hath shade far denser o'erhead
Than with thee, and his cones doth the pine from the height of his dark
    crown shed.

LACON.

Nay, lambskins here and a heap of fleeces beneath thy feet   50
Shall be strewn thick, softer than sleep : but an odour, even less sweet
Than reeks from thy carcase, floats all round from the skins of thy goats.
With white milk brimmed shall a wide bowl there be set by mine hand
For the Nymphs, and therebeside shall another of sweet oil stand.

COMATAS.

If thou come to this woodland bower, the soft fern here shalt thou
    tread,
And the marjoram's fragrant flower ; and under thy feet shall be spread
Goatskins—far softer be these than lambskin of thine or fleece !
Eight pails will I set there, crowned for Pan with the milk's white foam ;
Eight bowls shall be ranged around of honey adrip from the comb.

LACON.

Contend thou then even there : there sing thou, for aught I care ! 60
O keep thine oaks, and crow from thy native midden !   But whom
Shall we have for the umpire !—O that Lycopas the herdman would come !

COMATAS.

Nothing of him will I ; but a man hard by do I see,
Yon woodcutter slashing the heather, and binding in faggots together :
Unto him, if thou wilt, let us cry—I know him, Morson is he.

LACON.

Let us cry to him then.

COMATAS.

Call thou.

LACON.

Ho, stranger, draw nigh for a space,
And hearken.   At strife be we now, touching who in the herdfolk's lays
Is the better.   Good sir, do thou be, O Morson, of partial mind
Nowise herein unto me, nor to him be thy favour inclined.

COMATAS.

Yea, for the Wood-maids' sake, nor of me be a partisan,   70
Dear Morson, nor yet do thou take unjustly the side of this man.
Lo, yonder sheep doth he tend for Sibyrtas of Thurii :
For Eumaras of Sybaris, friend, this flock of goats feed I.

LACON.

'Fore heaven, of thee did one crave whether these to Sibyrtas belong,
Or whether the flock, thou knave, be mine ?—beshrew thy tongue !

COMATAS.

Most worshipful, truth alone is uttered in all that I say.
I brag not of wealth not mine own : but thou art a railer aye.

LACON.

Sing, sing, if thou hast one stave ! Let the hapless man get back
To town from the brink of the grave—from thy tongue's pestiferous clack !

COMATAS.

Not Daphnis the Singer's strain is more by the Song-queens prized   80
Than mine : fair she-goats twain unto them have I sacrificed.

LACON.

Ah, but Apollo greatly loves me : for him do I rear
A fair ram, now that his stately feast Carnean is near.

COMATAS.

The goats that I milk have borne all twins, save two that have one.
Cries a girl, looking sweetest scorn : " Poor wretch, art thou milking
    alone ? "

LACON.

Aha, but with cream-cheese maunds nigh a score doth Lacon fill,
And clasping his love in his hands amid flowers he hath all his will.

COMATAS.

At the goat-herd the apple, that's cast for love, Clearista throws,
As he drives his she-goats past, and sweet, sweet kisses she blows.

LACON.

But to Cratidas' flower-face this shepherd's heart is lost.   90
O'er his neck with a careless grace the shining curls are tossed.

COMATAS.

Your dog-rose may not vie, your anemone cannot compare
With the one queen-rose, that high o'er the garden-wall shines fair.

LACON.

Nor are mountain apples at all compared with acorns : there grows
Bitter husk over these from the gall-oak : sweet as honey are those.

COMATAS.

I will give to mine own dear maid a cushat soon from the wood,
From her nest mid a juniper's shade ; for there doth she sit and brood.

LACON.

Soft wool, that the weaver may make him a mantle, of me shall be borne
Unto Cratidas, for whose sake the dark-fleeced ewe shall be shorn.

COMATAS.

Hence from the wild-olive sprays, my bleaters. Here, where the hill 100
Slopes steeply up, may ye graze 'neath the tamarisk-bushes your fill.

LACON.

Conarus, hence with thee from the oak ! Cynaetha, away !
On the eastward slope feed ye with Phalarus, who doth not stray.

COMATAS.

A mazer of cypress-wood stands in mine hut, and a bowl is there
Carved by Praxiteles' hands : they are kept for a maiden fair.

LACON.

A hound, staunch friend of the fold, a throttler of wolves, is my gift.
For my love is he trained : he will hold in chase fierce things and swift.

COMATAS.

Ye locusts, lightly springing o'er the fence of my vineyard-close,
Waste not my vines, now the clinging tendril lushly grows.

LACON.

Ye grasshoppers, mark ye not how I gall yon goatherd-swain ?   110
Even so do ye gall, I wot, the reapers of the grain.

COMATAS.

The bush-tailed foxes I hate, which prowl by Micon's wall
Watching his grapes, and wait to devour them at evenfall.

LACON.

And the chafers I hate : like a cloud that drifts on the wind they fly ;
O'er the figs of Philondas they crowd, and consume them greedily.

COMATAS.

Dost remember my trouncing of thee, and thy face of a mowing ape,
As thou clungest to that oak-tree, and didst writhe and twist to escape ?

LACON.

That I remember not, clown, but when Eumaras tied
Thee up, and dressed thee down—ha, that in my mind doth abide !

COMATAS.

There is some one, Morson, now, who is stung !   Thou hast noted it ? 120
To an old crone's grave go thou ; pluck squills for thy poor crazed wit !

LACON.

He winced, good Morson, then ! Thou dost see him for shame flush red !
Go thou, dig cyclamen by Hales, for thy cracked head !

COMATAS.

With milk let Himera flow for water : Crathis, with wine
Rosily run ; may there grow on thy reeds the fruit of the vine !

LACON.

May Sybaris' fount at my prayer well honey : at dawn may the maiden,
Plunging her waterpot there, draw it forth with honeycombs laden !

COMATAS.

My goats crop clover sweet, and the goat-wort's golden crown,
Tread lentisk under their feet, and on arbute leaves lie down.

LACON.

But for these my ewes here groweth the honeywort's balmy stem 130
For their cropping : abundantly bloweth the rock-rose here for them.

COMATAS.

I love not Alcippe : she caught not my face her hands between,
Nor lovingly kissed, when I brought her a fair ring-dove yestreen.

LACON.

But I love Eumedes above all other tenderly ;
For I offered a pipe to my love, and a sweet kiss guerdoned me.

COMATAS.

That jays should with nightingales vie, O Lacon, is nowise right,
Neither hoopoes with swans : but thine eye is evil, thy soul all spite.

MORSON.

Let thy singing, young shepherd, end : Comatas, Morson to thee
Awardeth the lamb for thy prize ; so, when thou dost sacrifice
To the Nymphs, straightway do thou send a goodly portion to me. 140

COMATAS.

That will I, by Pan do I vow ! Leap, he-goats, toss the horn
Through all mine herd ! Lo now, how I laugh loud laughter of scorn
Against yon shepherd of sheep, yon Lacon ; for now have I gained
The lamb from him ! I will leap heaven-high for the triumph attained.
My she-goats, be ye of good cheer, my horned ones : to-morrow I wash
You all in the pool where the clear-welling waters of Sybaris plash.
Ho there, I will cudgel thy coat, if I see thee leaping again
On one of mine herd, he-goat of the white skin, ere I have slain
My lamb to the Nymphs—lo there yet again !—may Comatas be turned
To Melanthius[1] straight, if I spare thee the cudgelling thou hast earned ! 150

1. A goat-herd in the *Odyssey*, who is put to death with tortures, for treachery to his lord, Odysseus.

IDYLL VI.

Two young herdmen chant a dramatic sketch, " The Song of the Cyclops."

DAMOETAS and Daphnis the neat-herd, driving their flocks o'er the leas,
In one spot chanced to meet : russet-bearded was one of these,
Half-bearded the other ; and they, in the noon of a summer day,
Where forth was a fountain springing, sat down and chanted the lay.
It was Daphnis began the singing, as the challenger doth alway.

DAPHNIS.

Galatea is pelting thy flock, Polyphemus, with apples, and thee
For a laggard in love doth she mock, O goat-herd, alluringly ;
And thou lookest not toward her, O dear ! O dear ! but sweetly dost sound
Thy pipe there sitting—lo here, yet again is she pelting thy hound,   [10
Thine attendant who watcheth thy sheep ; and he barks in a fury-storm
Looking seaward : the bright billows leap asunder ; revealed is her form
As she flits through the shallows mid dashing of shore-waves softly
    plashing.
Take heed lest he rush on the fair one as forth she comes from the sea,
Lest he snap at her ankles, and tear her sweet limbs piteously !
Lo there, how she wantoneth, as, light on the summer-wind's breath,
Dry thistledown dances free o'er the plain in the sunglare hot ;
And from him that loves doth she flee, and pursueth who loves her not ;
And she staketh her all on a throw ; for oft in the glamour-light
Of love do foul things show, Polyphemus, fair to the sight.

He ended, and sweetly outrang Damoetas' voice, and he sang :   20

DAMOETAS (*as Polyphemus*).

" I saw her—by Pan, did I spy when she pelted my flock, nor me
She eluded, nor my one eye, my jewel, wherewith I shall see

To the end—that boder of doom, yon Telemus,[1] let him bear
His hateful oracles home, for his children to treasure them there !
But, all to torment her, I meet her glances with one look never ;
But I feign that I know one sweeter and fairer.   In jealousy's fever
She hears, and she pines—O Apollo !—she rushes forth of the sea :
For her rival she peereth through hollow caves, through the flocks on the
    lea.
I tarre my dog slyly to bay her ; but when she was loved of me,
He would whimper softly, and lay his head upon her knee.   30
Messengers many, it may be, will she send, when she seeth me still
Doing this : at my gate all in vain shall they wait, till she swear that she
    will
Here in mine island array me a bridal-couch 'neath the hill.
For surely I am not of face ill-favoured, as slanderers say ;
For of late on the sea did I gaze, when hushed in calm it lay ;
And beautiful showed my beard, and my one eye starry-bright—
After my judgment—appeared : my teeth more snowy-white
Than marble of Paros gleamed : yea, I spat thrice solemnly
In my bosom, so goodly I seemed, to avert the evil eye :
For thus did the ancient dame Cotyttaris teach me her lore,   40
To Hippocoon's harvest who came to pipe to his reapers of yore."

  So made Damoetas an end : then kissed he Daphnis his friend.
And he gave him a pipe, and the other to him gave a flute for guerdon :
So Daphnis piped, while his brother herdman fluted the burden ;
And the calves were dancing anon o'er the soft grass unto the strain.
So neither the victory won, but unvanquished abode they twain.

    1. The prophet who foretold to Polyphemus that Odysseus would blind him.

IDYLL VII.

In this poem, in which some scholars maintain that the poet and his friends are masquerading as country-folk, the narrator tells of the doings at a harvest-home, and of the singer they met on their way thither.

WITH me once Eucritus to the Hales-stream fared down,
And Amyntas joined him to us, as forth we passed of the town ;
For the Feast of the Lady of Corn Phrasidemus and Antigenes
There had arrayed, sons born to Lycopeus ; noble were these
As any of ancient name ; for their lineage of Clytia came
And of Chalcon, who smote with his foot, and uprose Burinna's spring.
His knee to the rock did he put hard-thrusting, and lo, a ring
Of poplars and elms drew over the fountain their arches of shade,
With their cool green leafage to cover the Wood-nymph's hallowed glade.
   We had won not half-way yet, and Brasilas' tomb in sight   10
Not yet had appeared, when there met us another wayfaring wight,
And a true man he, by grace of the Muses, Cydonian of race ;
And the name of him Lycidas, a goat-herd ; and none had deemed,
Which beheld him, that other he was, for a goat-herd of goat-herds he
     seemed.
For over his shoulders was hung a goatskin, close in the hair,
Shaggy and tawny, and clung the scent of the rennet there ;
And folded about his breast, by a plaited girdle clasped,
Was an old worn mantle-vest, and a cudgel his right hand grasped,
Wild-olive, a twisted staff.   In his eyes a quiet smile
Shone ; flashed his teeth as the laugh on his lips played all the while : 20
" Simichidas, whither," he cried, " through the noon dost drag thy feet,
When sleeps on the hot wall-side the lizard himself for the heat,
When the crested larks lie hidden, and none soars over the mead ?
Art thou to a banquet bidden, who hastenest thus, or with speed

Is a townsman's winepress winging thy feet, that stone after stone
Like a bird from the path flies singing, struck by thy hurrying shoon ? "
    And in answer to him I spoke : " Dear Lycidas, all men say
That thou among all herd-folk that can skill on the pipe to play,
And of all the reapers, art best ; and for this are our hearts aglow ;
And yet might I stand the test against thee—-to my mind is it so.   30
To a harvest-feast are we going, for certain our friends array
To Demeter of stole fair-flowing a festival this day
From the firstfruits of all they have reaped ; for the Goddess with plen-
    teous store
Of sheaves of the barley hath heaped this year their threshing-floor.
Come then—for the day and the way are thine and mine, O brother—
Chant we the pastoral lay ; each haply shall gladden other.
Sooth, mine is a clear-ringing tongue of the Muses, and all folk say
That I am the prince of song : do I lightly believe them ?—nay !
By Zeus, not I ! for, I trow, the mighty singer, whose home
Is Samos, Sicelides—no, nor Philetas can I overcome.   40
Should a poor frog strain his throat in song with cicalas to vie ? "
    Artfully spake I : the goat-herd, with laughter-litten eye,
Said : " Lo, this staff for thine own do I give, forasmuch as thou art
A plant which Zeus hath sown, and truth is enshrined in thine heart.
For, even as I detest the artificer who essays
High as Oromedon's crest a mansion of men to upraise,
So the birds of the Muses I hate, who weary themselves in vain,
Cackling early and late, to rival the Chian's strain.
Come, let us our voices upraise, in song to each other replying,
Simichidas—nay, friend, see, if this be well-pleasing to thee,   50
I will sing thee the last of my lays, which I made on the hill-side lying.
(*Sings*.)
    Fair voyage to my heart's delight unto Lesbos, alike in the days
When the South-wind, questing the flight of the Kids, holds surges in
    chase,
And when stormy Orion uplifts feet high on the Ocean's face—
If my sweet from the Love-queen's fire pluck Lycidas, so let it be,
For hot is the flame of desire for my love that consumeth me.

Peace then shall the halcyons inweave with the waves, till the wide sea
    sleeps,
And the south-wind and east, that doth heave sea-tangle from fathomless
    deeps—
The halcyons, dearest they to the Sea-maids hyaline
Of all the birds whose prey is won from the heart of the brine.   60
Fair winds, calm waters befriend my belovèd sailing on
Unto Lesbos, and so at the end may a happy haven be won !
I, when that day dawns bright, will with anise or roses be crowned,
Or a garland of violets white shall about my temples be bound.
Then out of the bowl the wine of Ptelea for me shall flow,
As at ease by the fire I recline, and the beans in the embers shall glow :
With asphodel, endive, I'll heap, and with parsley's curled green crown,
A soft bed elbow-deep, whereon to lay me down.
I will kiss the goblet, and drink to my darling overseas
With lips that cling to the brink of the cup that I drain to the lees.   70
And from shepherds twain, the one of Acharnae, shall flute-notes ring,
And the other Lycopia's son ; and there shall Tityrus sing
How the heart of Daphnis broke with love for a stranger-maiden,
How he roamed the mountains, and oak-trees over him sorrow-laden
Sighed requiems—all which grow where Himera's waters flow ;—
How he faded as wastes a snow-wreath on long-ridged Haemus' breast,
Or on Athos, or Rhodopé's brow, or on uttermost Caucasus' crest ;
And shall sing of the dungeon-chest, and the herdman pent there of old
Alive, by the mad behest of a tyrant evil-souled ;
And shall sing how the flat-faced bees came up from the meadow-leas 80
To the scented cedar, and fed him with honey of delicate flowers,
Because that the Muses had shed on his lips sweet nectar-showers.
O blessèd Comatas, to whom befell that happy fate—
In the chest wast thou lapped for thy tomb, yet on thee did the brown
    bees wait :
Thou, feasted on honeycomb, through the spring didst endure thine
    estate.
O that with living men thou hadst dwelt through this lifetime of mine !
On the hills had I herded then those fair she-goats of thine

Gladly, and hearkened thy singing, while thou under oak and pine
Hadst lain, sweet notes outringing from thy lips, Comatas divine ! ''
   So sang he, till died on the ear his strain.   Then spake I in turn   90
Unto him : " O Lycidas dear, many songs so sweet did I learn
Of the Nymphs, when along the lone hill-side I followed the herd,
That thereof unto Zeus's throne may rumour have borne some word :
Of them all, my chiefest lay, wherewith I will honour thee now,
Is this—give ear, I pray, for the Muses' friend art thou :
   (*Sings.*)
" On Simichidas breathed was the blessing of the Loves, his heart's dreams
    cling
About Myrto with love as caressing as the love of his goats for the Spring.
But Aratus, a friend in all things dearest to me who sing,
His heart to a fair one is thrall : Aristis knoweth the thing,—
A good man, the best in the land ; even Phoebus himself might desire   100
That he by his tripods should stand, and strike to his praise the lyre !—
He knows how with love's hot yearning Aratus' bones are burning.
O Pan, who hast taken to thee in possession the lovely lea
Of Homole, draw to his arms the love of his heart unbidden,
Be he thrall to Philinus' charms, or of one whose name yet is hidden.
Dear Pan, if thou grant this prayer, may the boys of Arcadia spare
To scourge with whips of the squill thy shoulders and sides, in the day
When they win not so much as they will in the hunt of the flesh of the prey.
But if naught our petition avails, may thine itching skin be frayed,
Scratched, scored by thine own mad nails, and of nettles thy couch be
    made !   110
And in bitter midwinter-tide on Edonian heights, and where
Flows Hebrus, mayst thou abide, unscreened from the frozen Bear,
And in summertide range with thy flock where the uttermost Aethiops are,
'Neath the Blemyans' sun-scorched rock, from glimpse of the Nile afar !
From Hyetis' sweet spring come, and from Byblis' waters fair,
Ye who dwell in the craggy home of Dione of golden hair,
O Eroses, faces flushing like apples crimson-blushing,
Smite ye !—your vengeful darts at the witching-sweet one send ;
Smite, for the conqueror of hearts no pity hath shown to my friend !

                                 D

Yet ah, over-ripe is the pear, and already the women say :   120
' O cruel beauty, beware, for thy bloom fast fadeth away ! '
Come away, Aratus ; no more let us sentinel yonder door
With feet that know no ease : let the cock's shrill challenge invite
Some other forlorn one to freeze in the chill of the dawn's dim light.
Let Molon alone be racked, and groan in a hopeless fight !
But our portion be careless quiet : let a crone breathe o'er us a spell
That shall still the heart's wild riot, and evil enchantments repel."
    So sang I : and, still with the old sweet smile, he gave unto me
That staff, for a pledge that enrolled in the Muses' Guild were we.
Then leftward he swerved, and was gone on the path unto Pyxae that
        led ;   130
But rightward I turned me, and won Phrasidemus' rich homestead,
And with me was Amyntas the fair, and Eucritus : so did we there
On earth-strewn couches deep with the odorous lentisk recline,
And rejoicing lay on a heap of the fresh-stripped leaves of the vine.
Over our heads on high did many a poplar wave,
Many an elm : hard by, from the Wood-maids' hallowed cave
The water was streaming, falling, murmuring dreamily ;
And from shadowy boughs aye calling their ceaseless challenge-cry
Sun-scorched cicalas screamed : far off, amid tangled thorn
Hidden, the dwarf owl seemed in sleep to mutter and mourn.   140
The larks and the finches were singing, ring-doves moaned soft and
        low :
Bees yellow-banded were winging their flight o'er the brook to and fro.
Of the golden summer-tide and her gifts breathed all the air.
Pears rolled to my feet, by my side in the green grass scattered there
        were
Apples uncounted ; and store of the wildwood fruit bowed low
Earthward the branches that bore the amethyst-purple sloe :
And the cap from the wine-jar we tore that was sealed four years ago.
    Nymphs, warders of Castaly's Spring, of Parnassus' twin crag-towers,
Did Cheiron the ancient bring such bowl as this of ours
Unto Pholus' cave in the rocks, and set it by Herakles ever ?   150
Or was that strong lord of flocks, who dwelt by Anapus the river,

Polyphemus, who hurled uprooted mountains at ships on the deep,
By such nectar beguiled, that he footed the dance mid the folds of his
    sheep?
Nymphs, had they ever such draught as for us ye deigned to pour,
Such as we by the altar quaffed of the Queen of the Threshing-floor?
Oh to plant yet again on the heap of her corn the great fan, while she
    stands
Smiling, with sheaves and the sleep-laden poppies filling her hands!

IDYLL VIII.

This sketch of a singing contest between two boys is affirmed by divers learned scholars to be " certainly not by Theocritus," for reasons which, mutatis mutandis, would as conclusively prove that " The Jolly Beggars " is not by the author of " The Cottar's Saturday Night."

As Daphnis the fair from the vale drave kine up the long green steep,
There met him, as telleth the tale, Menalcas feeding his sheep.
The down on their cheeks that day was golden in life's young spring :
On the pipe were they cunning to play, and skilled were both to sing.
And first unto Daphnis spake Menalcas with scornful eye :
" Thou warder of lowing kine, wilt meet me in minstrelsy ?
My song shall outrival thine by as much as pleaseth me."
Thereat did Daphnis make to his challenger proud reply :
" Thou tender of long-fleeced sheep, who dost waste on the pipes thy breath,
Never triumph o'er me shalt thou reap, though thou sing thyself to death ! " [10

MENALCAS.

This issue—art willing to try it ?   Wilt hazard a stake thereon ?

DAPHNIS.

To try it ?—yea, that will I ; and a stake will I set to be won.

MENALCAS.

What then shall we hazard, to make a fair match one against other ?

DAPHNIS.

A calf is my gage : thou stake me a lamb tall-grown as his mother.

MENALCAS.

Never a lamb ; for my father is stern—O, the deed should I rue !—
And my mother : at even they gather the sheep, and they number them
    through.

DAPHNIS.

What then wilt thou stake ?   Say what shall be set for the victor's meed.

MENALCAS.

A beautiful pipe which I wrought, of nine stops, reed by reed,
With white wax fastened in line, all level above and below.
Even this will I stake, it is mine ; but the goods of my father—no !   20

DAPHNIS.

I too have a pipe like thine, of nine reeds set in a row
With white wax fastened in line, all level above and below.
But of late did I fashion the thing, and aching still is my finger ;
For the reed, as I fashioned it, split, and deeply the keen edge bit.
But who shall give ear as we sing ? who judge 'twixt singer and singer ?

MENALCAS.

Full well shall he serve us, I wot, if we call him, the goat-herd yonder,
He whose dog with the broad white spot barks now at the kids that would
    wander.

To the goat-herd then did they cry, and he heard them, and straight
    drew nigh.
Then sang the lads ; for the goat-herd consented to judge in the singing.
First sang—so fell the lot—Menalcas of voice clear-ringing :   30
Then Daphnis' voice, in a burst of the music of herdfolk, rang
In answer. Menalcas first uplifted his voice, and sang :

MENALCAS.

O dales and rivers, ye seed of the Gods, if Menalcas ever
    Sang in his minstrelsy a strain well-pleasing to you,
His lambs for his heart's ease feed ye ; and if unto dale or river
    Daphnis with his calves draw nigh, the like boon count ye his due.

DAPHNIS.

O well-springs and pastures of sweet-springing herbs, if the passionate
    pleading
Of the throat of the nightingale thrill through Daphnis' voice and reed,
O fatten this herd at his feet ; and if, to the pastures leading
    His flock, come Menalcas, fulfil ye the measure of all his need.   40

MENALCAS.

Here do the she-goats bear ever twins, and the ewes : overflowing
    With bees, the glad hive hums, nor otherwhere tower so tall
The oaks, as where Milo the fair sets foot.   In the hour of his going
    Haggard the shepherd becomes, and wither the pastures all.

DAPHNIS.

Spring in the land !—green meads, deep udders with milk distended
    Are all around, and strong is the life in our fosterlings,
Where Naïs the lovely treads : but ah, if away she wended,
    Herdmen and kine ere long should be sun-dried, bloodless things.

MENALCAS.

Goat, lord of the harem white, ye kids with your innocent faces,
    Hie hence to the forest deep, where shadowed the streamlet steals : 50
Tell Milo there, when ye light on my love in the shady places,
    Even gods have been shepherds—for sheep did Proteus of old herd seals.

*   *   *   *   *   *[1]

MENALCAS.

Not mine be the lands of a king, no treasure of gold for me, love,
    Nor feet that can speed in the race more swiftly than breezes can flee !
But beneath this rock will I sing, in my arms enfolding thee, love,
    Watching our sheep as they graze by the side of the Western Sea.

1. One or more stanzas have been lost here.

DAPHNIS.

A curse unto trees is a storm, a drought unto flowing waters,
 A springe to the birds of the sky, unto wildwood beasts a net ;
To a man a maid's sweet form—O Father Zeus, earth's daughters
 Have held thee in thrall : not I alone have been love-beset.   60

So each against other they sang in stave for stave, they twain,
Till Menalcas' voice outrang at the last in the crowning strain :—

MENALCAS.

Spare thou my lambs, wolf, spare the ewes of the flock : wrong not
A boy, for that under the care of a child be too many, I wot.
Star-tail, my dog, what, asleep ?—and so soundly ?—fie on thee, fie !
Shame that in slumber so deep a lad's flock-warder should lie !
Feed on, my ewes ; refrain not from cropping the tender blade
To your fill ; ere ye weary, again shall its mantle have thickly arrayed
The mead.   Up ! feed on still, till your udders be heavy, till these
Your lambs have enough, till I fill the plaited crates with cheese.   70

Then Daphnis with notes clear-ringing uplifted his voice in singing :—

DAPHNIS.

Me from her cavern the maid of the married brows espied
Driving my calves through the glade—" Thou art fair, thou art fair ! "
     she cried.
But never a word did I cast of merry gibing back,
But with down-dropped eyes I passed along mine appointed track.
O sweet is the heifer's lowing, and sweet her breath, and sweet
To lie 'neath the blue by the flowing water in summertide heat.
Of the oak-tree are acorns the pride, rose-globes of the apple-tree ;
Of the cow, 'tis the calf at her side, of the neat-herd, his kine on the lea.

So sang they stave for stave, till his sentence the goat-herd gave :   80
" Daphnis, sweet is thy tongue, and thy voice is witching-sweet.
It is better to hearken thy song than of honey in comb to eat.

Receive thou the pipe, the meed of the singer's victory :
If but one thou wilt teach, while I feed my goats, of thy songs unto me,
This poll-horned goat will I pay for fee of thy lesson given ;
She filleth the milk-pail aye brimming over even by even."
   Then as glad was the boy—and high he leapt, as uplifted on wings,
Clapping hands for the victory—as a fawn by her mother that springs.
But the heart of the other died like a smouldering lamp, sore shaken   90
With grief, like the grief of a bride when her childhood's home is forsaken.
And highest was Daphnis' head thereafter the shepherds among ;
And Naïs ere long did he wed, while yet was the life in him young.

IDYLL IX.

A shepherd tells how two young herdmen sang to him the rival pleasures of summer and winter, and how he rewarded them with gifts and song.

SHEPHERD.

SING, Daphnis, a song of the neat-herds! Let thy voice first outring—
Yea, sing thou first, and his sweet song then shall Menalcas sing.
First bring ye the calves to the cows, and mate ye the barren ones yonder,
Let all together browse, and through the coppices wander;
Yet not from the herd let them stray: then sing thy song unto me,
Thou first; and Menalcas' lay shal answer in melody.

DAPHNIS.

Sweet is the young calf's call, and sweetly the heifer loweth;
The pipe rings sweetly withal, and sweetly mine own song floweth.
By the cool brook-side have I spread me a couch of leaves; it is piled
With fair skins stripped from the white calves hurled from the hill-brow's
      height,   10
The while on the arbute they fed, by a gust of the south-wind wild.
So the flaming summer skies I regard with the selfsame scorning
As when two young lovers despise a father's or mother's warning.
  Thus to me Daphnis sang; and Menalcas' strain thus rang;—

MENALCAS.

O Etna my mother, I dwell in a cavern fair to see;
Neath the rifted rock is my cell, and the wealth of the pageantry
Of dreams have I—many an ewe, and she-goats many are mine:
'Neath my head and my feet do I strew their fleeces whereon to recline.
Paunch-puddings be hissing there on the oak-billets, acorns dry
Glow mid the logs' red glare; and of winter less reck I   20
Than for walnuts the toothless will care when the furmety-bowl stands by

I clapped mine hands to acclaim them, and gifts I gave to the two,
Unto Daphnis a staff—the same in my father's orchard grew
Self-shapen so truly and well that a craftsman could find no flaw ;—
And a lovely spiral shell to Menalcas—that prize I saw
Mid Icarian rocks, and I drew therefrom its tenant, and won
A feast for five,—and he blew a merry blast thereon.
Hail, Pastoral Muses ! show now forth to the light my song
Which I sang, by the side as I lay of the shepherd-boys that day :—
May the liar's blister grow never up on the tip of my tongue !　　　30
　　" To cicala cicala is dear, and ant is dear unto ant,
And hawk unto hawk ; but near to mine heart is the Muses' chant.
With this may mine whole house ring !　Not sleep is sweeter to me,
Nor the sudden burst of the spring, nor so dear are the flowers to the bee,
As the Muses are dear to my soul.　Whomsoever with glad good will
They befriend, no Circe's bowl can avail to work him ill."

IDYLL X.

A love-sick reaper and his sturdy heart-whole fellow-labourer sing, the former a love-ditty, the latter a harvest-song.

MILO.

Thou a labourer !—pitiful wight ! Thou oaf, what ails thee now ?
Thou canst not drive forthright thy swath, as once didst thou,
Nor press on thy neighbour's heels in the reaping, but laggard thou art
As a ewe from the flock, when she feels in her foot a sharp thorn's smart.
What wilt thou be when the sun is low—nay, at midnoon heat—
Who, when scarce is the day begun, dost cleave not the ranks of the
    wheat ?

BATTUS.

  Thou whom no reaping can tire, thou son of the flint-rock's race,
Hast thou never known desire ?—never longed for an absent face ?

MILO.

Never !—what unto labouring men are the grapes that be hung too high ?

BATTUS.

And it never befell thee, then, all sleepless with love to lie ?   10

MILO.

No—heaven forbid ! " It is bad that of meat should the dog taste
    merely."

BATTUS.

But I, oh Milo my lad, I have loved for eleven days—nearly.

MILO.

He draws from a wine-cellar's store !—even vinegar's scarce with me !

BATTUS.

And the plots before my door unweeded since sowing-time be !

MILO.

But which of the lasses, then, smote thee ?

BATTUS.

Polybotas' maid :
To Hippokion's reaping-men but of late on the flute she played.

MILO.

His sin has found him out !—'tis the judgment thou long hast been
    seeking !
That grasshopper-girl, thou lout, all night in thine arms will be creaking !

BATTUS.

Thou mockest at her I would woo !—not Plutus alone is blinded ;
So is Eros the reckless too.   Mock *him* not, as one high-minded !   20

MILO.

Not I am mocking him.   Raise thy sickle, and lay corn low ;
Then strike up a love-song in praise of thy maiden : more pleasantly so
Shalt thou toil.   Yea, in old-time days hast thou trolled songs many,
    I trow.

BATTUS (*sings*).

Muses Pierian, to sing the Sylph-girl help your singer ;
For transfigured is everything whereon ye lay but a finger.

Bombyca, my winsome bird, on the " gipsy-wench " let them rail—
At the " sun-browned skeleton " gird—*I* call thee honey-pale.
Dusk, too, are the violet's hues, and the flower with the words of grieving ;
Yet of all blooms first do they choose even these for their garland-
    weaving.

The goat to the clover flieth, the goat by the wolf is sought ;   30
The crane in the share's track prieth ; I, I am for thee distraught !
Oh that mine were the treasure untold of Croesus in legend related !
Unto Love's Queen, fashioned in gold, we twain would be dedicated,

> Thou, holding thy pipes in thine hand, and an apple, or rose it may
>   be ;
And in festal attire would I stand, and in new shoon goodly to see.
Bombyca, my winsome ! thy feet are as ivory dice light-ringing ;
Thy voice is a love-dream ; sweet are thy ways beyond my singing !

Milo.

> So of beautiful songs was a lout a maker !—we knew it not, we !
How featly he measured out his rhythms of melody !
Alas for my beard—so long, yet no such wisdom is mine !   40
Tush !—mark thou this, the song Lityerses made, the divine !

(*Sings*) Harvesting Song.

Demeter, Harvest-queen, O Lady of Sheaves, may the corn
This day be easy to win, and full be the ears it hath borne !

Knit up, ye binders, the sheaves, lest a passer-by should say :
" Dawdlers be here, nay, thieves—they have never earned their pay ! "

To the north-wind turn ye still the stalks' cut ends, or to west
Let them look ; so the grain shall fill out fullest, and ripen best.

Threshers of corn, refrain you from taking the noontide sleep :
Lightliest then from the grain and the stalk doth the winged chaff
    leap.

Ye reapers, begin when the crested lark from his sleep doth awake ;   50
Let your work cease when he is nested : siesta at noon shall ye
    take.

The frog's life, that should be mine, my lads : not a whit doth he care
For a butler to dole out his wine—he hath liquor enough and to spare.

Thou miserly steward, come, boil better the lentil-stew—
And beware lest thou cut thy thumb when splitting a cress-seed in two !

   That is the song to shout to lads that are reaping the corn.
Thine ?—sing for a lullaby, lout, thy starveling lays love-lorn
When thy grandam turns her about in her bed at the breaking of morn !

IDYLL XI.

A consolatory poem to the poet's love-crossed friend, the physician Nicias.
It takes the form of " philosophy teaching by examples."

NOWHERE is a medicine found that may cure, O Nicias, love—
No salve that can slide through his wound, no balm ye may sprinkle
    above—
Not one, save the Muses' strain : it is soothing and sweet, to my mind,
Beyond all that men may attain—but ah, not easy to find !
And this canst thou well divine, in the healer's craft who art wise,
And art dear to the Muses Nine, above all men dear in their eyes.

   The Cyclops, our neighbour, consoled his days with minstrelsy,
When he loved, Polyphemus of old, Galatea the Maid of the Sea,
When round temple and mouth was the gold of youth outcropping free.
He loved not with presents of flowers, or of apples, or locks of hair,   10
But with madness wrecking his powers : for naught beside did he care.
Self-shepherded oft his sheep to the fold from the pasturing came,
From the grass thick-springing and deep ; but he sang Galatea's name
On the weed-strewn beach by the sweep of the surge with wasting frame
From the dawning grey, while his breast burned aye with the arrow of
    flame
Shot, heart-stinging, keen, by the Cyprian Queen with unerring aim.
Yet he found this salve for his pain : on the high cliff's brink sat he,
And he sang this manner of strain, looking out on the heedless sea :
" O Galatea the White, why fling thy lover afar ?—
O whiter than curds to the sight, O softer than young lambs are !   20
As a calf in thy frolicsome mood, bright-skinned as a grape rose-hued !—
Yet thou comest and hauntest my sleep when slumber enfoldeth me here,
But art gone when slumber's bands are unlocked by invisible hands,
Yea, fliest as flieth a sheep that hath spied the grey wolf near.

In love with thee fathom-deep, O maiden, I fell on the day
When thou cam'st at my mother's side, and wouldst gather the hyacinth's
    pride
Where it purpled the mountain-steep, and I was thy guide for the way.
From the hour that I saw thee, and ever thereafter, I cannot forbear
From loving thee ; no, and shall never—by heaven, not a whit dost thou
    care !
I know, O loveliest, how it befalls that from me thou hast fled—   30
'Tis because of the shag-haired brow across my forehead spread :
From ear unto ear doth it go like a hedge from side to side ;
And but one eye peeps from below, and my nose is flat and wide.
Yet—such as I am let me be—I pasture a thousand kine,
And the milk that they yield unto me !—there is none upon earth like mine.
Nor in summer nor autumn do cheeses fail from my stintless store ;
And when bitterest winter freezes, my full crates still run o'er.
Yea, never a Cyclop can skill to play on the pipes like me :
Sweet-apple, my love, I still in my songs join me and thee
As I sing in the hush of the night.   Eleven fawns, thine, do I rear—   40
Each one hath a brow-crescent white—and four young whelps of the bear.
Oh come thou with me !—never doubt but thy bliss thereby shall be
    more !—
Leave the cold grey sea stretching out unsatisfied hands to the shore !
More pleasantly here in the cave wilt thou fleet the dreamy hours :
Hereby green laurels wave, and the dark slim cypress towers :
Here dusk-leaved ivy flickers, the vine sweet-clustered swings :
The cold stream babbles and bickers, which Etna from snow-fed springs
From under his mantle of trees down sends me, a draught divine.
Who would choose in the stead of these a home mid the waves and their
    brine ?
And if haply I seem to thine eye over-shaggy for maiden fair—   50
In my cave oak-billets lie, and fire 'neath the ashes is there.[1]
Ah, though thou shouldst burn out all my soul, I would bear it from thee—
Yea, or my one eye-ball, most precious of treasures to me.

---

1. Alluding to the primitive method of shaving, by singeing.

Ah me, that my mother bare me not with fins bedight !
I would plunge to thy sea-grot, and there would I kiss thine hand, my
    delight,
If I might not thy lips.   I would bring unto thee of the lilies white
Or the poppy soft, with its ring of petals crimson-bright—
Nay, this in the summer doth blow, and that in the winter weather ;
Therefore I could not bestow on my love the twain together.
Now, maiden, now and here will I learn the swimmer's lore,   60
If so be that a stranger draw near with his ship to mine island-shore,
That so I may learn what bliss is in haunting the depths of the sea.
Galatea, come forth the abyss ; and thereafter forgotten of thee—
As of me, sitting here on the rock, it hath been—be the homeward way ;
But consent thou to follow the flock, and to milk them at close of day,
And to pour sharp rennet therein, and the shapely cheese to mould.
O, my woe is my mother's sin !—her only to blame do I hold !
For never, not once, hath she spoken for me kind word unto thee,
Though day by day heart-broken she sees me with misery.
Ha, I will tell her my brow and my feet in feverous anguish   70
Throb : so shall she suffer, I trow, the pain wherein I languish !
O Cyclops, Cyclops, whither have thy poor wits taken wing ?
Go, plait thee thy baskets, and hither the young shoots gather, and bring
Food to thy lambs : a mind far sounder so shalt thou find.
Milk thou the ewe that is by thee ; why follow that which doth fly thee ?
A new Galatea in days to come shalt thou find, and a sweeter.
There is many a maiden that prays me at gloaming-tide to meet her ;
And all laugh low for delight, whensoe'er to their prayers I give ear.
Plain is it that great in the sight of the world on land I appear."

    Polyphemus with song so lured his lorn love home to the fold,   80
And more heart's ease he procured than by feeing physicians with gold.

IDYLL XII.

The passionate outpouring of a lover, to whom " joy cometh in the morning."

You are come in the dawning grey, belovèd! Three nights have
    passed—
With longing do men in a day grow old—are come at the last!
As sweeter than winter is spring, as the apple doth sloes excel,
As the fleece of a ewe is a thing richer far than the young lamb's fell,
As fairer a young girl's face than a thrice-wedded dame's doth appear,
As bounds with an airier grace the fawn than the calf, as clear
Above all bird-song outrings the nightingale's note when she sings,
So sweet and so rich and so fair have you come!   To your arms have I run
As the wayfarer runs from the glare to the shade when high is the sun.
Ah, may Love's balmy breath upon us twain evenly blow,   10
That we may be theme of the praise of the bards of the oncoming days—
" How with love more strong than death into one did their two souls
    grow!
For the one was a ' Heart's Desire '—sweet name in Amyclae framed;
And the other a leal true ' Squire '—so is he in Thessaly named;
And with equal love did they burn—ah, that was the Age of Gold,
When love won love's return in the happy days of old!"
   Ah, would that, O ageless Immortals—ah, would that, O Cronos' Son,
When ten-score ages have fled, might tidings be brought to the dead,
Unto me, through Hades' portals, to the stream whence returning is
    none—
" Through the whole world still is the story of the hearts that together
    clung   20
An unforgotten glory wherever hearts are young!"
Ah well, the Abiders on High shall overrule, as they deem
For the best, all this: but when I call you the Beauty Supreme,
Not on the tip of my nose shall blossom the " perjurer's rose."

Yea, if e'er you have pained your lover, you have straightway healed the
  sore,
And have paid me back twice over, and left my cup running o'er.

Nisaeans of Megara-town, sea-kings, ever glad be your days
For the honour wherewith ye crown Diocles of Athens, your praise
Of your guest who of old laid down his life for a child of your race.
Around his tomb for this do the children yearly throng   30
And contend for the Prize of the Kiss when the spring is lovely and young.
Whosoever so sweetly bestoweth love's seal, that he passeth all other,
With garlands laden he goeth at eventide home to his mother.
Happy who sits throned there, Love's Umpire of Kisses decreed !
Oft must he put up a prayer unto bright-faced Ganymede
That unerring his lips may decide as the Lydian stone, when the gold
By the money-exchanger is tried, and the true from the false is told.

IDYLL XIII.

The Story of Hylas, an episode from the Tale of the Argonauts.

Not for us only was Love, friend Nicias, born, as we thought,
Whosoe'er of the Dwellers Above that Child into being brought,
Nor we were the first unto whom was the Vision of Beauty revealed,
Who are mortal, who know not the doom in the lap of to-morrow con-
    cealed.
Nay, also Amphitryon's son, that heart of steel, who unmoved
Abode when in rage rushed on him the lion,—he also loved
Young Hylas the winsome-sweet, of the clustering curls tossed wild,
And he taught him all things meet, as a father would teach to his child,
Whereby had himself waxed strong and brave, and renowned in song ;
Nor ever he left him—no, nor when Day was through mid-heaven pac-
    ing,   10
Nor when Dawn of the Steeds of Snow was up to the Gods' home racing,
Nor when cheep small fledgling things at the perch so high and afar,
While their mother is shaking her wings above the smoke-smirched bar.
All this did he, that so to his mind might the lad be trained,
Be a true yokefellow, and grow till the perfect man were attained.
    But when Aeson's son on the quest sailed forth of the Fleece of Gold,
And with Jason followed the best of the mighty men of old,
The chosen of tower and town, even all that were good at need,
To Iolcos the man of renown through many a desperate deed
Came, son of the heroine-queen, Alcmena of Midean blood ;   20
And beside him was Hylas seen where Argo the fair-benched stood,
She which leapt through the Crags Dark-blue, and grazed them not as
    they clashed,
But through them and onward flew, till up deep-flowing Phasis she dashed :
O'er the gulfs like an eagle she passed, and the Rocks left rooted fast.

At the Pleiads' rising-tide, when up to the hills from the plain
Go the pasturing lambs, and the pride of the spring is beginning to wane,
Then passed that flower divine of heroes down to the shore,
And 'twixt Argo's bulwarks in line they sat them down at the oar ;
And the south-wind blew, and they passed on the third day Hellespont's
 stream ;
And within Propontis they cast the anchor, where ploughshares gleam 30
As open the furrows wide 'neath Cianian oxen's feet.
Forth to the strand did they stride ; they made ready the eventide meat
Thwart by thwart : one bed thereby they strewed for their crew ;
For beside them a broad mead spread, where all that they lacked for it
 grew.
So they mowed them the flag's sword-edge, and the tall-growing galingale-
 sedge.
 And bright-haired Hylas with speed for the water of supper departed
For his own lord Heracles' need, and for Telamon steadfast-hearted—
For these twain ever would share one board in their banqueting—
And a vessel of bronze he bare ; and soon had he marked a spring
In a low-lying spot, and around it were rushes in plenty growing : 40
Swallow-wort darkened the ground, green maidenhair-tresses were flow-
 ing :
Lush parsley there was found, and the marsh-flower broadly-blowing.
In the midst of the woodland-mere did Nymphs their dances array,
The Sleepless Maids ; the fear of the country-side were they :
Eunice and Malis are here, and Nycheia with eyes of May.
The boy by the fountain bent him, the pitcher thereover he swung ;
To dip it therein he leant—lo, unto his hand all clung ;
For with love of the Argive child were the tender hearts of them all
Shaken with passion wild : through the dark flood down did he fall
Headlong, as flaming doth leap a star from the height of the sky 50
Headlong down to the deep, and shipman to shipman doth cry :
" Lads, reef ye the sail, for a gusty gale is drawing nigh ! "
Now on their knees did they hold that boy, the Maids of the Spring,
While he wept, and they fain had consoled him with soft love-whisper-
 ing.

Forth, anguish-racked for the lad, the son of Amphitryon went ;
And in Scythian fashion he had his bow in his hand ready-bent,
And his massy club, the same that is grasped in his grip evermore.
Thrice cried he on Hylas' name with his deep throat's lion-roar,
And thrice did the lost child hear : faint, thin was the voice that replied
From the water : albeit so near, from afar did it seem that he cried.   60
As a lion of splendid mane, who hath heard from far away
Mid the mountains a lost fawn plain, a lion greedy of prey,
From his lair to the feast rusheth out that he deemeth already spread ;
So the hero in anguish of doubt for the lad, and in tumult of dread,
Quested the forest about, and through trackless thorn-brakes sped.
How reckless is love !   On pressed he by thicket and mountain and glen,
Toiling and roaming—the quest of Jason was naught to him then !
   With her tackling aloft, by the shore waited Argo with all her crew ;
But at midnight the youths once more the sail to the deck down drew
Awaiting him.   Far apart was he roving in frenzy forlorn   70
At his wild feet's will ; for his heart by the tyrant Goddess was torn.
   With the Blessed is Hylas the Fair thus numbered : in bitter jest
By the heroes was Heracles there named " Truant to Ship and to Quest,"
Since to Argo of thwarts thrice-ten not true had he proved that day.
Yet afoot to the Colchian men and to Phasis he won his way.

IDYLL XIV.

A forsaken lover tells his friend the story of the quarrel that lost him his mistress.

AESCHINES.

ALL hail to Thyonichus !

THYONICHUS.

Hail, Aeschines, also to you !

AESCHINES.

How long since we last met thus !

THYONICHUS.

Is it long ? . . . What, wearing the rue ?

AESCHINES.

Out of suits with fortune am I.

THYONICHUS.

So for this are your bones so bare,
And your beard hangs raggedly, and unsleeked and unkempt is your hair.
In such plight hitherward came a Pythagorean but now,
Wan, barefoot, born and bred an Athenian—or so he said :
And lo, his complaint was the same, in love—with our fritters, I trow !

AESCHINES.

Ah, friend, you must still have your quip ! She flouts me, Cynisca
the fair !
Into madness unwares shall I slip !—'tis but crossing the breadth of a hair !

THYONICHUS.

Friend Aeschines, so are you still : cold yesterday, hot to-day,   10
Wanting all things with weathercock-will—well, what is the new whim ?
Say.

AESCHINES.

The Argive, and I, and the horse-couper Apis of Thessaly,
And, on furlough home from the force, Cleonicus—well, we three
To drink at my farm were met.   I had killed a suckling swine,
Two chickens withal ; and I set forth fragrant Bybline wine
Before them, four years stored, and sparkling as run from the vat.
There were truffles and snails on the board—O, a pleasant feast was that !
When our hearts grew merry with cheer, 'twas agreed that in pure wine all
Should drink unto each guest's dear, but the name must each first call.
So we call our names, and we drink like men : but she—not a name !   20
Though myself sat there !   You may think how my blood at the minx was aflame.
" Tongue-tied ! " one jested—" *you* sighted the wolf ! "[1]   " How witty ! " she cries ;
And her face flamed : one might have lighted with ease a lamp at her eyes !
There's a Wolf—ay, a wolf in truth !—Old Labas' son is he,
A lank-limbed, girl-faced youth—some think him comely to see !
For his worshipful love, good sooth, was she pining secretly !
Ay, a whisper that crept about had come to mine ears ere then ;
Yet I looked not into it—out on my beard !   Do I rank with men ?
And by this, as I said, were we well in our cups, we four, when the man
Of Larissa the mad fool, fell to singing ; and lo, he began   30
" My Wolf ! "—a Thessalian song : and Cynisca, what doth she,
But suddenly loud and long she weeps, more bitterly
Than a lost little maid of six years strayed from her mother's knee !
Then I—too well do you know me, Thyonichus—shot out my fist
Twice, on each temple a blow.   She twitched up her skirt o'er her wrist,
And was gone like the wind.   " Thou jade ! " I shouted, " art sick of me ?
Hast another with whom thou hast played more pleasantly ?   Hence with thee !

1. Alluding to the superstition that if a man was sighted by a wolf before he saw the animal, he became dumb.   Here it is implied that it was *she* who had sighted the wolf, and therefore had no excuse for being tongue-tied.

Cherish thy love !   O, thine eyes for his sake great apples are weeping ! ''
Fast as a swallow flies, for her young 'neath the eaves loud-cheeping
To bring back a morsel to feed the mouths ever hungrily crying—   40
Nay, faster still did she speed from her cushioned chair, forth flying
Through porchway and folding door, wheresoever her wild feet led,
To be seen, as they say, '' no more than a bull to the forest that's fled.''
  Since then it is twenty—and eight—and nine—then eleven days come—
Add two—then eleven up to date—two months in all is the sum
Since we parted.   I never shave—a policeman's a trimmer sight !¹
Wolf's everything now : that knave finds doors left open at night.
And I—I count not at all : in the pitiful '' poll '' is my place :
Like the wretched Megarians, I crawl at the very tail of the race !²
Could I cease but from loving, O that would bring all right at the last : 50
But, Thyonichus, now I'm the rat with his feet in the pitch stuck fast.
If for hopeless love there may be any cure, I cannot tell.
There was Simus indeed—his flame Epichalcus' daughter—the same
Was his age as my own : oversea he sailed, and he came back well . . .
I too will take service, will go overseas !   If I am not the first
Of soldiers, I'll prove, I trow, a fair one, by no means the worst.

THYONICHUS.

I would you had not been forsaken, had won the desire of your heart.
But if your resolve be taken, if fixed you are to depart,
For a free-born man the best paymaster is Ptolemy.

AESCHINES.

Ay, and as touching the rest, how fittest for freemen is he ?   60

---

1. Scythians—rough fellows with shaggy hair and beards—were employed as policemen.

2. The Megarians, hoping that their gifts to the oracle would gain them honourable mention, sent to Delphi to inquire which city was pre-eminent in Greece   The answer they received was :—

> Argos for soil stands first, and for goodly horses Thrace ;
> For fine men Syracuse, Sparta for women's beauty and grace ;
> But ye, O Megarians, attain not the third, nor yet fourth place,
> No, nor the twelfth : ye are nowhere, utterly out of the race.''

THYONICHUS.

Indulgent, a scholar, a lover, and genial to the core.
Keeps an eye on a friend, and, moreover, keeps an eye on a foe yet more :
Free-handed to all in largesse ; what you ask, he denies you never,
And he gives as a king gives—yes, but you must not be asking for ever.
If, then, it is good in your eyes o'er a strong right shoulder to fling
Your mantle in soldierly guise, and with feet unfaltering
Before the onset to stand of the foe's bold targeteers,
Away with speed to the land of Egypt !   The on-coming years
Soon silver our temples, and inch by inch to the chin Time's frost
Creeps.   Let us then not flinch from work ere our vigour be lost.   70

IDYLL XV.

Gorgo, an Alexandrian lady, calls, with her maid Eutychis, on her friend Praxinoe, whose maid is Eunoe, to take her to see the Festival of Adonis at the palace of King Ptolemy.

GORGO.

PRAXINOE in ?

PRAXINOE.

My dear ! at last ! I am here, quite ready.

GORGO.

It's a marvel I ever got here !

PRAXINOE.

Eunoe, a chair for the lady.

Fetch a cushion.

GORGO.

It does very well as it is.

PRAXINOE.

Sit down for a spell.

GORGO.

O why can't folks stop at home ? I scarce got hither alive !
Crowds everywhere aimlessly roam, and hundreds and hundreds that
    drive !
High boots here, and there regimentals—and oh, the road
Is endless ! 'Tis too far, where you have taken up your abode.

PRAXINOE.

That madman it was !—took flight to the world's end : hither he came,
Took a hole, not a house, that we might not be neighbours : his only aim,—
The jealous brute—is to spite us : it's like him, always the same .   10

GORGO.

Mind how you talk, my dear, of your husband—be careful, do,
When the little fellow is near !   How hard he is looking at you !
All right, Zopyrion, my pet !   She doesn't mean Pa, doesn't Ma !
He takes notice—it *is* early yet, by our Lady !   Pretty Papa !

PRAXINOE.

That "pretty papa" t'other day—though I *told* him to take special
    care,
Soap and rouge being wanted—away he goes to the shop, and there
He buys me—the booby, the great long looby brings salt, I declare !

GORGO.

Mine's like him, a waster—bought five fleeces yesterday, paid
Seven shillings apiece for—naught but dog-skins, old bags frayed
Into rags !   Good cash did he pay for trash !   Oh, the trouble it made ! 20
Well, come, get on your shawl and your mantle, and come with me
Away to Ptolemy's hall, to our rich king's palace, to see
The "Adonis."   I understand the queen has provided a show
Most splendid.

PRAXINOE.

Of course, "with grand folks everything's grand," you know.

GORGO.

What sights you'll have seen to report to the stay-at-homes !   Come,
    my dear !

PRAXINOE.

No hurry.   "The go-easy sort keep holidays all the year."
Eunoe, pick up your sewing !   Slut, leave it about, if you dare !
Those cats will always be going for a soft bed anywhere.
Wake up !   bring water, and quickly—first water !   She's brought soap-
    paste ![1]
Never mind, spread it on—not thickly like that, you creature of waste ! 30

---

[1]   Soap seems to have been sold, not in cakes, but in the form of paste or powder.

Pour over the water—don't splash ! You wretch, you are wetting my
    dress !
That will do. Well, I *have* had a wash—a treat for the Gods—such a
    mess !
Now, bring it to me—where is it ?—the key of the big clothes-press ?
(*Opens clothes-press, and puts on new dress*).

GORGO.

My dear, that dress, pleated full, becomes you indeed, I must say !
Do tell me—how much, when the wool came back from the loom, did you
    pay ?

PRAXINOE.

O, don't make me think of it !—more than eight pounds silver it cost !
And the work I put into it !—wore out my soul in the making, almost.

GORGO.

Well, it *is* a success ! It's all that heart could desire !

PRAXINOE.

                      Very kind
Of you. (*To Eunoe*). Now, bring me my shawl, and my hat—put it on
    straight, mind !
(*To the child*). No, I'm not taking chickie to-day—there's a bogey-horse
    —bites little boys !   40
Cry as much as you like—cry away ! I'll not have you lamed for your
    noise.
Now, let us be off. Nurse, take him, and play with the little one.
Call in the dog, and make the street-door fast when I'm gone.
(*They pass out into the street with their maids*).
O heavens, what a crowd ! How ever on earth shall we get through
This block ? They're like ants—you never could count, no, nor measure
    the crew !
Well, Ptolemy, really you've given us many reforms, I vow,
Since your father ascended to heaven : no burglars and pickpockets now

Pouncing on peaceable folks round corners, Egyptian style.
Nice rough practical jokes did they play, those lumps of guile,[1]
All birds of a feather, rowdies together, vile, all vile !   50
Dear Gorgo, what shall we do ?—war-horses, the king's own stud !
Dear Sir, I do beg of you, don't trample me into the mud !
O, see, how he's rearing, the bay !   How vicious !—don't rush on your
   doom,
Eunoe !—out of the way !—he'll be surely the death of his groom !
What a blessing I made him stay, that urchin of mine, at home !

GORGO.

  All right, Praxinoe, at last we're behind them ; they've all gone by:
On to parade they have passed.

PRAXINOE.

             I'm reviving again—O my !
Of horses and cold snakes I've had a horror, yes, from a girl.
Come, we must look alive.   What a crowd !   We'll be caught in the swirl
(*An old lady meets them*).

GORGO.

From the palace, mother ?

OLD LADY.

        Yes, my dears.

GORGO.

                 Is it easy to get   60
Inside ?

OLD LADY.

    The Greeks, by stress of trying, my pretty pet,
Got into Troy.   By dint of trying are all things done.   (*Exit*).

GORGO.

Quite an oracular hint—and therewith is the old dame gone.

---

   1. Referring to bands of roughs who, in pretended horse-play among themselves,
hustled and robbed people, and who had been sharply put down under the new police-
system.

PRAXINOE.

Women know everything—not excepting how Hera was wed.

GORGO.

O look, Praxinoe, what a crowd at the gates on ahead !

PRAXINOE.

Tremendous ! Take hold tight of my arm ; and to Eutychis cling,
Eunoe, with all your might : don't lose us for anything !
In, all in a bunch, we go—hold on to us, Eunoe, you !
O dear ! O dear ! I know that my scarf is torn in two,
Gorgo. (*To stranger*). For heaven's sake, as you wish for happiness, 70
My good sir, please do take some care of my poor dress !

GOOD-NATURED STRANGER.

I will do all I can—but here 'tisn't much.

PRAXINOE.

What a crowd—packed tight,
And pushing like pigs !

GOOD-NATURED STRANGER.

Don't fear, madam ! Now we are through all right !

PRAXINOE.

And may *you* be all right, this year, and the next, and through all life's
    span,
For your care of us, kind sir ! (*Exit Str.*) What a nice, considerate man !
Where's Eunoe ?—jammed in the crush ! Push, O you donkey, push !—
Right ! " All safe now inside ! "—as he said who had locked out his bride.[1]

---

1. Various interpretations have been given of this passage, owing to the circumstance
that ἀποκλάξας may mean "shut out," or "shut in," and that νυός is any female
relation by marriage :—

  1. As the absent-minded bridegroom said, when he had locked out his bride.
  2. As the jealous husband said, when he had safely locked up his bride.
  3. As the bridegroom said, when he had locked his bride in with himself.
  4. As the husband said, when he had locked out his mother-in-law.

GORGO.

Praxinoe, here !—such a treat !   Look first at these broideries.
How filmy !   How perfectly sweet !   They would do for the Gods in the
    skies !

PRAXINOE.

O Goddess of Spinning, who were the weavers that fashioned these ?   80
And who were the artists who drew those patterns ?—such truth and
    such ease !
Like real live creatures they stand, and like live things move on the curtain
As if breathing, not woven by hand !   Well, man is a wonder, for certain !
And himself—how lovely here he lies on his silver bed,
And how sweet do his cheeks appear with the first soft down overspread,
Adonis !—the dear ! thrice dear, dear even among the dead !

IRRITABLE STRANGER.

You nuisances, do be still !—you are everlastingly gabbling
Like turtles !   They're fit to kill one with that broad brogue they are
    babbling !

GORGO.

Good heavens ! who are you with your hectoring ?   What if we chat
    as we choose ?
Order your servants !   Lecturing ladies of Syracuse !   90
We, let me tell you, Sir Clever, are from Corinth, the ancient city,
Like Bellerophon—wasn't he Greek ?   Good Peloponnesian we speak ;
And if Dorian women may never talk Dorian speech, it's a pity !

PRAXINOE.

O honey-sweet Proserpine, save us from masters more than our due !
One's enough !   I'm not *your* slave, to be stinted and starved by you !

GORGO.

Praxinoe, hush !   She's about to sing the " Adonis Psalm "—
The prima donna—came out from Argos : she took the palm
For the " Dirge " last year ; so she, I'm perfectly certain, will sing
Something fine.   She's beginning, you see, with her smiling and posturing.

THE SINGER.

(The " Adonis Hymn " to Aphrodite).

O Queen, who lovest thy nest in Golgi, Idalium's hold,   100
And Eryx's craggy crest, Aphrodite who sportest with gold,
Lo, from Acheron's river eternal the Hours of the down-shod feet
In the twelfth month from the infernal abodes bring Adonis the sweet.
Slowest-winged of the Heavenly Ones be the Hours ; yet with yearning
    sore
Be they hailed by all earth's sons, for with blessing they come ever-
    more.
O Child of Dione, the story tells how a mortal hath been
By thee in immortal glory arrayed, Berenice the Queen,
When by thee the ambrosia-rain through the breast of the woman was
    poured.
O Lady of many a fane, and by many a name adored,
For thy joyance her daughter, fair as was Helen, Arsinoe,   110
Now decks thine Adonis with rare and radiant bravery.
All fruits by his side are displayed that the trees' high branches bear,
And the dainty " gardens " arrayed in baskets of silver are there ;
And from vases with gold overlaid breathe orient scents on the air.
All cates that women invent and on kneading-platters mould,
When with white wheat-flour they have blent bright blossoms manifold,
And have mingled the honey sweet, and the limpid oil, to appear
Like birds upon pinions that fleet, or like creeping things—they are here.
And fresh leaf-bowers, hung over with that soft anise-screen,
Are built for him : everywhere hover Child-Eroses over the green ;   120
Like fledgling nightingales trying their new-born wings in the trees,
From branch unto branch ever flying and fluttering, so seem these.
Oh the ebony !—oh the gold !—oh eagles of ivory white !
With the Gods' cupbearer behold how they wing unto Zeus their flight !
Oh the crimson coverlets strown o'er the couches, softer than sleep !—
As Miletus herself will own, and the tenders of Samian sheep.
Lo, a second couch yonder whereon Adonis the fair shall repose—
For Cypris one, and one for Adonis with arms like a rose.

F

Years eighteen, perchance nineteen, that sweet boy-bridegroom hath told :
Soft are his kisses, I ween ; on his lips is the down's pale gold.   130
Good night unto Cypris our Queen, and the lover her arms enfold !
But to-morn will we go forth all, while glistens the dew on the land,
And will bear him to where waves fall with gentle plash on the strand ;
And we, with unbraided hair, vests dropped to our ankles, revealing
To the sun bright bosoms bare, will upraise this chant clear-pealing :—
" Belovèd Adonis, alone of the Demigods, as they tell,
Dost thou visit both Acheron and earth.   Such fortune befell
Nor Atreides, nor Aias, by whom death stood when with rage he was torn,
Nor Hector, of Hecuba's womb the eldest of twice ten born,
Nor Patroclus, nor Pyrrhus who came from Troy home over the brine,   140
Nor the Lapiths of olden fame, nor Deucalion's ancient line,
Nor whom Argos her kings did acclaim, nor the Pelopids half-divine ! "
Be propitious, Adonis dear, and for next year gracious be thou !
Then again will we welcome thee here with such joy as we welcome thee
          now.

GORGO.

My dear, it's beyond poor me !   Happy woman, to know so pat
Such a great song !   Thrice happy she with a lovely voice like that !
Well, well, back again must we get.   My lord is dinnerless yet ;
And the man's all vinegar then—he is quite unapproachable.
Good-bye, dear Adonis, and when you return, may you find us well !

IDYLL XVI.

In this poem, which is a bid for the patronage of Hiero, king of Syracuse, the poet names his poems " The Graces," probably because great poets had associated the Graces with the Muses (as Euripides, in " The Madness of Hercules," l. 673), or even identified them with them (as Pindar, Olympic Ode xiv).

To the Daughters of Zeus is it given evermore, and to bards evermore
To chant the Dwellers in Heaven, the deeds of the Heroes of yore.
The Muses are Goddesses ; sweetly from them Gods' praíses shall ring ;
But mortals are we, and meetly of mortals shall mortals sing.
  Ah, who of all that abide beneath the Dawn's grey wing
To our Graces hath e'er flung wide with gladsome welcoming
His doors, and will not send them guerdonless thence as they came ?
Ah, home barefooted they wend with downcast eyes of shame.
Then me do they bitterly chide who had sent them on fruitless quest,
And weary and listless-eyed in the depths of the empty chest,   10
Which is ever their dwelling-place when gainless home come these,
They bow the despairing face low down on the comfortless knees.
Who now is generous-souled ?   Who befriendeth the giver of fame ?
None !—men care not, as of old, that the bard should extol their name
For noble deeds : unto gold are they captives whom greed overcame !
The purse with the hand they grip ; ever watching for lucre are they :
They will scrape not the rust from the tip of a nail, to give it away.
Ask—straightway the answer is given : " More near than my cloak is my
    skin.
I must look to mine own : of Heaven let poets their guerdon win !
Who asked for a new singing voice ?   Is not Homer enough, the divine ?
He is the bard of my choice who expects not a stiver of mine."   [20
  Alas for you !   What boots it, the gold that hoarded lies
Within—wealth barren of fruits for the man, in the sight of the wise ?

Spend somewhat for thy soul's good : the poet's song do thou guerdon ;
Give somewhat to them of thy blood ; make lighter the poor man's
    burden ;
Ever to altar and fane of the Gods pay sacrifice meet ;
Forget not to entertain the stranger, but kindly entreat
At thy board while he wills to remain, and speed his parting feet.
To the Muses' interpreters, whom they have hallowed, honour give,
That, when hidden in Hades' gloom thou liest, thy fame may live,   30
That renownless thou mayest not mourn by Acheron's cold flood,
Like some poor hind with worn hands chafed by the spade's rough wood,
Unto poverty's heritage born from sires of ignoble blood.
    In King Antiochus' halls, 'neath the roof of Aleuas of old,
To underlings many and thralls was the monthly pittance doled ;
Calves by the thousand were driven to the pens of Scopas' line
Loud-lowing even by even, with thousands of hornèd kine.
Upon Crannon's pasture-mead were sheep unnumbered tended
By shepherds for Creon's seed, of whom was the stranger befriended.
Yet of all these joy had they none, when once they had gasped life's
    breath
        40
Away, and o'er Acheron were borne by the Ship of Death ;
But forgotten, and all that store from the griping fingers torn,
Through age after age evermore had they lain mid the dead forlorn,
If the Ceian of manifold-ringing voice, the master of song,
Had not, by his lyre far-flinging their praises the ages along,
Unto these given deathless fame, and to their swift steeds renown
Which from hallowed contests came home bearing victory's crown.
    Of the champions of Lycian race, of the Priamids' lion-like hair
Who had heard, or of Cycnus' face as the fairest maiden's fair,
Had their battle-cries never been rolled down the years by the singers of
    old ?
        50
Nor Odysseus—what though he fared through homeless months six-score
To the world's end, what though he dared to pass through Hades' door
Alive, though out of the gory den of the Cyclops he won—
Had gained him abiding glory : the swine-herd Eumaeus had gone
Down to oblivion, and none of Philoetius the neat-herd had found

Any record : no deeds had been told of Laertes the king great-souled,
Had the songs of Ionia's son not made all these renowned.

From the Muses' Fountain the shower of fame over men is shed ;
But the living heirs devour all hoarded wealth of the dead.
Yet ah ! like toil flung away in counting the waves on the strand,   60
Which the wind and the heave of the grey sea onward hurl to the land,
Or as washing in shadowed pool a sun-dried brick is vain,
So fails thine appeal to the fool who is smitten with greed of gain.
Let him go his way : let a river of wealth o'er his manhood roll,
And let him be slave for ever to the greed that strangles his soul !
But for me, be a good name mine, and the love of my fellow-man ;
All wealth in mules they outshine, in all horses that ever ran.

I am seeking a man to whose door I may come, a welcome guest
Led by the Muses ; for sore are the ways to the bard in whose breast
Deep-counselling Zeus's Daughters, the Muses, ne'er set up their rest.   70
Not yet Heaven wearies of leading the months and the years in their
    courses,
And the sun's wheels oft shall be speeding yet after flame-footed horses :
And yet shall a Hero be found who will cherish the poet's strain,
A man of such deeds as were wrought by Achilles and Aias, who fought
Where Ilus the Phrygian's mound yet stands upon Simois' plain.

Already the sons of Tyre upon Libya's uttermost spur,
Where quenches the sun his fire, with thrilling hearts are astir.
Now, couched for the conflict, the spear do the sons of Syracuse wield ;
Now doth the strong arm bear the weight of the linden shield.
In the midst of them Hiero, brave as the heroes of old time, now   80
Girds him for battle, and wave dark plumes o'er his gallant brow.
Zeus, Father glory-crowned, O Lady Athena, hear,
And, Maiden, thou, who dost hold with the Mother, from days of old
The Ephyran city renowned, by Lysimeleia's mere ;
From our Island-home may the foe, by grim fate driven, be tost
Over waters Sardinian, that so from a remnant of that great host
Their wives and their children may know the doom of their dear ones lost.
Then free may the old homes stand to their olden abiders again,
All towns that a foeman's hand had levelled with dust of the plain.

Our fields may we plough, and reap their increase : in thousands untold 90
On the herb of the field may our sheep grow fat, and may fold unto fold
Bleat o'er the plain, while the homing kine, as they throng the ways,
Warn wayfaring men through the gloaming to hurry onward apace.
May the fallows be broken for sowing, what time the cicala, eyeing
The shepherds that toil in the glowing heat, mid the tree's shade crying
Sits on the topmost spray : may the spider's filmy snare
Over armour be woven, and may none name the war-cry there !
But may Hiero's fame on high from the lips of singers soar ;
O'er the Scythian sea let it fly unto where that rampart of yore,
By a Queen reared broad and vast, was knit with the asphalt fast.   100
I am one : many others there are whom the Daughters of Zeus hold dear ;
And they all be fain to sing of Arethusa the spring,
And of Sicily's folk, and their war-king Hiero, lord of the spear.
   Eteocles' daughters divine, who loved Orchomenus once,—
That burg of the Minyan line, once hated of Thebe's sons,—
While unbidden I am, let me bide at home, but with confident breast
Let me haste, with the Muses beside me, to such as will welcome the
        guest.
Nor, Graces, you will I leave : never blessing to men befell
Which from you they did not receive : with the Graces aye may I dwell !

IDYLL XVII.

In this panegyric of Ptolemy Philadelphus, the poet undertakes the formidable task of idealizing that king's incestuous marriage with his own sister, Arsinoe.

LET Zeus be the first whom we sing ; on his name let the last notes die,
Whensoever, ye Muses, outring your hymns to the King most high.
But foremost of men let the name be chanted of Ptolemy ;
Last, midmost, our theme be the same, for of all men chiefest is he.
    When the heroes of ancient days, sons' sons of the Lords of Heaven,
Wrought noble deeds, for their praise were royal singers given.
Let me—for in me doth the breath of inspiration burn—
Sing Ptolemy.   Hymns do the Deathless for glory-guerdon earn.
    When to Ida the forest-crowned goes the woodman axe in hand,
In doubt he gazeth around where trees unnumbered stand ;   10
And I—what first shall I chant ?—such glories there are untold
Which the Gods unto this king grant, of all kings noblest-souled.
    In the might of his sires no deed there was that he could not achieve,
Ptolemy, Lagos' seed, whatsoever his heart should conceive
Of counsel and kingly rede such as none other wit could weave.
Him too hath the Father holden in honour of Gods ever blest ;
And in Zeus's palace a golden mansion, the place of his rest,
Is built : to his bright abode his forerunner hails him away,
Alexander, who crushed like a God the splendour-turbaned array.
And, wrought of the adamant-stone, there standeth facing these   20
The steadfast-stablished throne of the bull-slayer Heracles :
And there with the Heavenly Ones doth he sit at the endless feast,
And rejoiceth in brave sons' sons with joy evermore increased,
Seeing Zeus hath taken away old age from their every limb,
And immortal henceforth for aye are the children descended from him.
These twain by descent be divine from the Heracleid mighty-souled,
So that both in the glorious line of Heracles' sons be enrolled.

When with odorous nectar the heart of the Hero is satisfied,
And he riseth up to depart from the feast to the bower of his bride,   [30
Then his bow to the one he giveth, and the quiver beneath it that hangs ;
And his club the other receiveth, with its knots like iron fangs.
To the bower ambrosial of white-footed Hebe bear they on
These weapons, escorting the might of Zeus's bearded son.
　　Berenice the world-renowned, amid all wise women her praise
Was pre-eminent—how she crowned with joy her parents' days !
Yea, on her fragrant breast Dionaea, who hath Love's Bowers
In Cyprus, lovingly pressed those hands like lily-flowers,
Whence never was bride, as they tell, that so ravished her lord with her
　　　love
As she, by the magic spell round Ptolemy's heart that she wove.
And on him did she bestow love loyaller yet ; and so   40
Fearlessly might he bequeath to his sons his sovereign sway,
When the hour drew nigh when death to his bride's bower called him away.
But the loveless woman—still for a stranger her heart is afire :
Children she hath, if she will, but not sons like to the sire.
Aphrodite, thou who didst win mid the Goddesses pride of place
In loveliness, for this Queen didst thou care : by thy special grace
Berenice the fair crossed never Acheron's river of woe ;
Thou didst snatch her away, or ever she came to its leaden flow,
Ere she looked on the awful face of the Pilot of Spirit-land,   [50
In thy temple didst give her a place, and thy sceptre didst lay in her hand.
She is kindly to all earth's sons, she inspires them with love wherein
Is no torment, and love-sick ones assuaging of anguish win.
　　O Argos' dark-browed daughter, thou barest to Tydeus a son,
Diomedes, a lord of slaughter, the hero of Calydon ;
And Thetis the deep-bosomed gave Achilles the spear-renowned
To the Aeacid Peleus ; but thee, O Ptolemy, warrior crowned,
Berenice the glorious bare unto Ptolemy, warrior-king,
And thy nurse was Cos the fair, who received thee, a new-born thing,
Of thy mother, when bright on thine eyes shone light of thy first dayspring.
On the Helper in Travail-pain, on Eileithyia, she cried,   60
Antigone's daughter, in strain of the pangs of travail-tide ;

And lo, of her grace was she there, and oblivion of every pang
She poured o'er her limbs at her prayer, and from her a dear son sprang,
His sire's true image.   A cry of joy from the Isle Cos brake,
And her hands clasped lovingly that new-born babe, and she spake :
" Child, bliss be thy portion undying !   May I be honoured of thee
As of Phoebus was Delos lying in her dark-blue sphere of sea :
On the Hill Triopion's crest may the selfsame honour rest,
And do thou such glory accord to the Dorian abiders near
As Rhenaion obtained from Lord Apollo who held her dear."   70
    So cried the Isle : from a cloud far up rang answering cries—
Zeus' eagle, crying aloud, the bird of boding, thrice.
O yea, Zeus gave that sign !   Right dear unto Cronos' son
Are heroes of royal line, and more than all that one
Whom he loves from the birth : his hand of the treasures of earth is full :
He ruleth o'er many a land, o'er the uttermost seas doth he rule.
    There be countless lands far-spread, and countless nations therein
From the soil by heaven's rain fed the wealth of its increase win ;
But of these none yield such store as Egypt, the plain lying low,
When the hard clods crumble before the wide Nile's overflow.   80
And of cities of men toil-skilled hath none so many as he,
For therewith is the land fulfilled : therein be hundreds three,
There be thousands three withal, there be thrice ten thousand arrayed,
Twice three, and the sum of all by thrice nine cities is made.
And Ptolemy mighty of heart over these hath sovereignty :
Of Phoenice he carved him a part, and the best of Araby,
And of Syria ; and Libya's folk, and the Aethiops swarthy of face,
And Pamphylia, bow 'neath his yoke, and Cilicia's warrior race :
His sway do the Lycians own, and the Carians, lovers of war,
And the Isles through the Mid-sea strown, forasmuch as his galleys are 90
The best o'er the great deep flying : yea, every land and sea
And the rivers seaward-sighing be ruled by Ptolemy.
Horsemen he hath enow, and many a targeteer ;
Clashing and flashing they go in splendour of battle-gear.
    All kings doth he outweigh in prosperity's balances,
Such wealth flows day by day into that rich palace of his

From every hand ; and their toil in peace do his people ply ;
For upon Nile's teeming soil no foot of an enemy
Hath trod, nor our hamlets have rung to the shout of a hostile band :
No mailèd raider hath sprung from his swift ship down to our strand   100
With lawless design to harry the kine of Egypt-land ;
Such a warder hath in his care her broad plains far and near,
The king of the golden hair, the lord of the quivering spear.
And with diligent heed doth he ward whatsoever his sires of yore
Possessed, as is meet for a lord of men, and he addeth yet more.
Neither useless lieth his gold in his palace, for aye increasing
Like the hoards that with toil manifold ants pile unresting, unceasing ;
But a goodly portion the splendour-gleaming temples receive ;
For the firstfruits aye doth he render, and gifts beside doth he give.
Full many a gift oversea unto mighty kings he sends,   110
And to cities his bounty is free, and lavish to loyal friends.
Never cometh a bard to the singing-contests in Bacchus' praise
Who hath skill in the song clear-ringing a voice inspired to raise,
But a guerdon worthy his lay he wins of our lord the King,
And the priests of the Muses aye King Ptolemy's praises sing
For his bountihead.   What crown of beauty is more of worth
For the wealthy, than high renown among all the sons of earth ?
This only to Atreus' son remaineth ; but all that prey,
All treasures of Priam, won from his halls in the triumphing day,   [120
To the bourne whence returning is none they have fleeted in darkness away.
   He only of all that have gone before, and of all whose feet
Yet leave warm imprint upon the trampled dust of the street,
Hath reared fanes incense-steaming unto mother and father, and there
Hath set their statues gleaming with gold and ivory fair,
That the help of these may be near unto all on the earth that abide.
The thighs of many a steer on their altars crimson-dyed
In sacrifice burned have been, as the months have swept around,
By him and his stately Queen, than whom no bride hath been found
Nobler, whose arms enfold a new-wedded lord in his hall ;
For she loves him with love whole-souled, who is brother and husband
        withal.   130

Yea, too, in the selfsame wise that holy bridal of yore
Joined twain, the Lords of the Skies, whom Rhea's majesty bore,
What time one marriage-bed for Zeus and for Hera arrayed,
By the hands myrrh-scented was spread of Iris the Goddess-maid.
All hail, O Ptolemy King ! Of the Demigods art thou one,
And so thy praise will I sing in a strain to be scorned of none
In the days to be—but thine excellency is of Zeus alone.

IDYLL XVIII.

The Bridal-chant sung at the marriage of Helen and Menelaus.

In Sparta in far-off days, in the halls of the bright-haired king,
Stood, crowned with the hyacinth's grace of freshness, a maiden-ring
Arraying the dance in the hall in front of the new-decked bower,
Damsels queenly and tall, twelve, Sparta's noblest flower,
When Helen was wooed and won, dear daughter of Tyndareus she,
And bridegroom and bride were alone in love's dim sanctuary,
When all with one voice sang, and with woven paces beat
The time, and the hushed halls rang to their song and the fall of their feet :
" So early art gone to thy rest, friend bridegroom ?   How, can it be
That thy limbs be slumber-oppressed ?—or is sleep so dear unto thee ? 10
Or what, hadst thou drunken deep, ere thou castedst thee down on thy
    bed ?
Betimes, and alone shouldst thou sleep, O thrall unto drowsihead,
And have left yon maiden to play at her loving mother's side
With girls till the dawning grey.   What need for this haste ?   Thy bride
Will she still be, while day after day, and while year after year on-glide.
    Happy bridegroom !   A blessing, I trow, was breathed on thine en-
        tering-in
With thy rivals to Sparta, that thou thine heart's desire might'st win.
Thou hast Zeus to thy father, alone of heroes of birth divine,
For, by love's rites sealed thine own, the daughter of Zeus is thine.
    Of Achaia's daughters, none other treads earth so peerless as she : 20
If her babe be like to the mother, a marvellous child shall it be.
With her we grew up, and we ran girl-races with flying feet,
Each suppled with oil like a man, where the swirls of Eurotas fleet,
Twelve-score maidens, the pride of womanhood's spring each one ;
But, set by Helen's side, of all these perfect was none.
Lovely as breaketh the dawn, O Night, through thy star-studded pall,
As, when winter is over and gone, shines Spring's bright coronal,
So Helen the golden shone most lovely amidst of us all.

The glory of corn-land glows in the shocks that thickly stand ;
The glory cypresses are of the garden, the steed of the car ;   30
And the glory is Helen, the Rose of the World, of the Spartan land.
No spinner there is of whom a thread more rounded is spun ;
From between the beams of the loom fair-carven weaver is none
Who sheareth so close a warp from her shuttle's flashing play ;
No harper there is whose harp so sweetly rings to the lay
That she chants to the Forest-queen, or Athena of ample breast,
As Helen, whose eyes' star-sheen is the young Loves' darling nest.
    O loveliest, winsomest thou, a queen of the hearth thou art now !
But we with the dawning will speed to the course, to the leaf-shadowed
     mead,
And all flowers incense-breathing will we pluck for our garland-wreathing,
Ever thinking, O Helen, of thee, as the tender yeanling lamb   [40
Craves ever longingly for the ewe, for the teat of her dam.
For thee first, Helen, a wreath of the lotus, that low on the lea
Creeps, will we twine, and beneath the shade of a broad plane-tree
Will we hang it : a cruse will we take of silver ; the oil will we pour
Therefrom, for thy sweet sake, 'neath the plane upon earth's green floor.
Carved Dorian wise shall appear on the bark—that the passer-by
May read—this legend : " Revere me, for Helen's tree am I."
    Hail, bride ! Hail, groom, who hast won a mighty Sire in this hour !
May Leto—Leto whose son is a God, vouchsafe you a dower   50
Of fair babes ! Cypris from heaven send mutual love alway ;
And of Zeus Cronion be given you wealth that shall know not decay,
Which your kingly heirs to your sons through the years shall bequeath
     for aye.
Sleep now, and breathe through the night love each into other's breast :
But forget not with morning's light to awake from the dreams of your rest.
With the dawn will we come yet again, when the clarion of morning shall
     ring
From the bough where her herald will strain plumed neck and quivering
     wing.
    Hymen, rejoice o'er the twain made one, O Marriage-king !

IDYLL XIX.

How Love the stinger of hearts was himself stung.

Eros the Thief of yore was stung by an angry bee
As he rifled the golden store of her hive, and the tips pricked she
Of all his fingers : he leapt with the pain, on his fingers he blew,
He stamped on the ground, and he wept as to Aphrodite he flew,
And he showed her his hurt—" It is shame," he cried, " that so tiny a
     thing
As a bee, so puny a frame, should deal so grievous a sting ! "
Answered his mother, and smiled : " Are not thou and the bees alike ?
Full tiny art thou, my child, but deeply thine arrows strike."

IDYLL XX.

The complaint of a young country fellow, who was flouted by a city girl.

EUNICE, fain had I kissed her, but scornful laugh and flout
Mocked me ; and fiercely she hissed : " Begone from my sight, thou lout !
Wouldst kiss me, thou keeper óf kine, foul thing ?   I know not," she said,
" How boors give kisses : mine are kept for the gently-bred.
Never think thou shalt kiss my fair lips, not in a dream !   O nay !—
Thou, with that talk, that air !—thou, with thy clownish play !
O, dainty thy talk is ! " she sneered : " bright wit thou utterest !
How softly curled is thy beard, thine head how lovely-tressed !
Why, thy lips like a sick man's show, and black are thine hands to see ;
Foul is thy savour !—go ! flee hence ! pollute not me ! "   10
As averting defilement, thrice in her bosom-fold did she spit,
While the slow cold scorn of her eyes crept o'er me from head to feet.
Scorn puffed from her lips—O the sneer in her side-look, the bitter gibe
In her mincing and bridling, the jeer in her laugh no words can describe,
Her fine-lady laugh of disdain !—my blood boiled through and through :
Crimson I flushed with pain, like a red rose wet with dew.
She turned her from me, and was gone : but mine heart is with anger aglow
That I, " the Comely One," should be mocked by a wanton so !
    Answer me truly, brother shepherds, am I not fair ?
Hath some God made me another man before I was ware ?   20
For bloomed as a garden on me sweet beauty heretofore
As ivy clings to a tree ; it mantled my chin all o'er ;
And like soft curled parsley my hair around my temples streamed,
And a forehead as ivory fair above my dark brows gleamed :
Far brighter did mine eyes shine than Athena's eyes deep-blue :
More sweet was this mouth of mine than curded milk ; therethrough
Sweeter the song-flood rolled than the honeycomb's liquid gold ;

And sweetly my music ringeth, whether my lips be set
To the pipe, or my flute's throat singeth, or the reed, or the flageolet.
And the mountain-maidens call me beautiful, one and all ;   30
Yea, kisses full oft they gave ; but the city-girl kissed not me,
Nay, ran from the " neat-herd knave ! "   Alas, she hath heard not, she,
How a lovely neat-herd-lad mid the glens was the Lord of the Vine,
Nor knows she how Cypris was mad with love for a herdman of kine ;
And on Phrygian hills as a neat-herd she was : amid oakwoods dim
She kissed Adonis the sweet, and wailed mid the oakwoods for him.
And Endymion, who was he then but a neat-herd ?   Down to his side,
Where he tended in Latmos' glen his kine, did the Moon-queen glide,
And kissed him ; and spread was a mortal's bed for a heavenly bride.
For thine herdman thy tears still break forth, Rhea : didst thou not
    too,   40
O Zeus, for a herdboy's sake, as an eagle swoop through the blue ?
    But Eunice alone, even she, must refuse to the neat-herd a kiss !
Than Cypris, than Cybele, than the Moon-queen greater she is !
O Cypris, no more presume, or in town, or on mountain-steep,
To love thy love, for thy doom is alone through the night to sleep !

IDYLL XXI.

An old fisherman tells his companion his dream of a golden catch.

FRIEND, only by penury are the arts uproused from sleep ;
Taskmaster of labour is she : ay, tyrannous cares ever keep
The man that toils with his hands from taking of rest in the night ;
Yea, though oblivion's bands for a little encompass the wight,
Suddenly care's ghost stands by him, putting slumber to flight.

 Two fishermen old and grey on beds of the sea-moss dried
In a wattled cabin lay and slumbered side by side
Half-propped by the leafy wall ; and thereby were the tools of their toil
Strewn round—reed fishing-rods tall, and creels for the ocean-spoil ;
And there were the fish-hooks hung, lines, weels for the crab claw-cloven,10
Bait to which sea-weed clung, and labyrinth-traps rush-woven :
There were seines, two oars, and an old boat stayed on its props stood there :
'Neath their heads there were small mats rolled, rough garments their
  coverlets were.
Their wealth were these—nothing more—these all their revenues.
Their threshold had neither door nor watchdog ; they had no use
For any such thing : of their labour the warder was Poverty.
Anigh them was found no neighbour : the lazy-lapping sea
Before their straitened abode on the lone beach sighed afar.
Not yet in her mid-course rode the moon on her silver car,
When our fishers were smitten awake by remembrance of toil. From
  their eyes   20
The burden of sleep did they shake : out of phantasy speech 'gan rise :—

ASPHALION.

 Friend, all of a surety have lied, who have said that the hours of the night
Wax fewer in summer-tide, when Zeus brings long daylight.

Lo, countless dreams ere this have I seen ; yet the dawn cometh not !
Do I err ?—or what is amiss ?   Full long are the nights, I wot.

COMRADE.

Asphalion, thou needest not chide fair summer : she doth not slight
Her law, neither runneth she wide of her course : it is care doth smite
With his staff evermore upon sleep's thin door, and he lengthens thy night.

ASPHALION.

Friend, hast thou not some skill to interpret dreams ?   I have seen
Good ones, and have no will that thou have no share therein.   30
As we share our catches still, of my dreams thy share shalt thou win.
Who shrewdly the truth can hit, of dream-arreders best
Hath proved him : his mother-wit is of teachers prudentest.
Yea, leisure for talk have we—what else should he do, who lies
On a leaf-strewn bed by the sea with sleep-forsaken eyes,
Like an ass in a thorn-brake caught, like the city-hall lamp alight ?—
For they say that it slumbereth not.

COMRADE.

            Come, tell me thy dream of the night ;
If my wit can unfold to thee aught, thy trust will I then requite.[1]

ASPHALION.

I fell asleep yestreen, forspent with the toils of the sea—
Not heavy with meat, I ween !   Sooth, early diners were we,   40
And Sir Belly gat no hurt from his load, as thou know'st.   In my dream
I crouched on a rock all alert, and ever for fish did I seem
To be watching : the bait from the reed I swung and twitched in the deep.
Then a huge fish dartèd to feed on the morsel—as always in sleep
Bears fill the prophetic eyes of the hound, so fish fill mine—
And behold, fast hooked was my prize ; his blood was streaking the brine.
The reed that I held was bent to an arch by his rushes and twists :
Ay, a wrestle most vehement with the monster had my wrists !

---

1.   The text of this line is hopelessly corrupt.

" Can this weak hook of mine hold that huge fish ? " I thought.
He sulked : with a twitch of the line his wound to remembrance I
    brought— 50
Pricked—slackened—but no, he would run not, and so I pulled all taut.
I had won my prize !—to the shore a golden fish I drew,
Yea, plated with gold all o'er ! But a new fear thrilled me through
Lest Poseidon's cherished gem peradventure this fish might be,
Or had dropped from the diadem of the hyaline Queen of the Sea.
With delicate touch did I slip out the hook as I loosened its hold,
Lest haply the barb from his lip might rend and waste the gold.
By a noose slipped round his tail my prize to the shore did I hale ;
And I swore I would set foot never thereafter again on the sea,   [60
But would stay on the land for ever ; a king with my gold would I be.
The thought of it smote me awake. Now, friend, lay to thy wit :—
I am fearful for mine oath's sake, lest I haply am bound by it.

COMRADE.

Fear not ; by no oath art thou bound : the golden fish that thine eyes
Saw visioned, thou hast not found : naught else are dreams but lies.
If thou search yon fishing-ground—but waking, not sleeping !—the prize
Of thy slumber to thee may fall ; but a fish of flesh must content thee,
Lest thou perish of hunger, for all the golden dreams that are sent thee.

IDYLL XXII.

A Hymn to the Twin Brethren, in two parts : 1, the story of Pollux's victory in boxing : 2, the tale of Castor's fight with Lynceus.

OF the Sons of Leda we tell, and of Zeus the Aegis-king,
Castor and terrible Polydeuces, a lord of the ring
When the hide-bands round his fists were bound for the buffeting.
Twice, thrice to that stalwart pair do we raise the glory-strain
Whom the daughter of Thestius bare, Lacedaemon's brethren twain,
The Saviours—saviours of men in peril's sharpest stress,
And of frenzied car-steeds, when they charge through the red war-press,
And of ships that, when they defy the stars in the west that set,
Or that rise in the morning sky, by fierce storm-blasts are met
Which over the ship's prow curl a huge foam-crested sea,   10
Or high o'er the stern, or whirl it as their wild will may be,
And into the hold they hurl it, and bulwarks to windward and lee
Are shattered : hang from the mast the tackling and sail, all riven
In tangled ruin, and fast pour cataract rains from heaven ;
And the night cometh on, and the vast sea rings and roars 'neath the flail
Of the merciless-scourging blast and the rush of relentless hail.
Yet despite all this do ye draw from unfathomed abysses to land
Ships with their crews, when they saw death looming hard at hand.
On a sudden the winds have died, as oil is the face of the sea
All calm, and scattering wide doth the huddled cloud-rack flee ;   20
And flash into view the Bears, and between the Asses appears
Dimly the Crib, which declares all calm for the mariners.
O well-belovèd Two, for mortals' help so strong,
Horsemen and harpers are you, and wrestlers, and lords of song.
Of which the first shall I sing, Polydeuces or Castor ?—nay,
Of both shall my praises ring, and be first Polydeuces' Lay.

By this had Argo fled through the Clashing Crags Dark-blue,
Even snowy Pontus' dread sea-gorge, had won safe through ;
And she came to Bebrycia, who bore the men from the high Gods sprung.
From her bulwarks forth to the shore then strode by the ladders hung 30
From the ship on either hand those heroes down to the strand.
Under the wind's lee there they tread the deep soft sand,
And their couches of leaves they prepare, and they blow up the touchwood-
    brand.
But with Castor the Chariot-king Polydeuces the sparkling-eyed
Alone went wandering from their hero-comrades aside.
On the hill-side marvelling they gazed on the trees thick-growing,
And a smooth cliff saw, and a spring from beneath it gushed ever-flowing
And with water pure overstreaming its rims, and therebelow
Like crystal and silver gleaming did the shimmering pebbles show
From its depths : there were pines uptowering near from the earth's green
    breast,   40
White poplars, and planes embowering, and cypresses lofty-tressed ;
There were flowers sweet-scented, dear to the downy-bodied bees,
That, when springtide's waning is near, bestar the meadow-leas.
But a monstrous man sat here in the sunglare, dreadful to see ;
By buffeting fists each ear had been battered hideously.
His Titan chest and his vast back domed and bossed uprose
Iron-fleshed, like colossus cast and moulded by hammer-blows.
On his massive arms rose mounded muscles beneath the curve
Of the shoulder, like pebbles rounded amidst the swirl and swerve
Of a torrent that rolled them and flung them through eddies that madly
    boiled ;   50
And over his back was hung and around his neck was coiled
A lion's tawny fell by the paw-tips roughly tied.
Unto that grim sentinel Polydeuces the champion cried :

POLYDEUCES.

Joy to thee, whoso thou be !   What folk possess this shore ?

AMYCUS.

Joy !—how should I joy, when I see men never seen before ?

POLYDEUCES.

Fear not : no reivers be come, nor the sons of reivers, here.

AMYCUS.

I fear ?—thou wert better dumb than hinting to me of fear !

POLYDEUCES.

Take offence at a word !—art a brute, or a man of arrogant brow ?

AMYCUS.

I am such as thou seest.   My foot upon *thy* land tramples not now.

POLYDEUCES.

Nay, come thither : so shalt thou go with guest-gifts back to thy land. 60

AMYCUS.

Gift me no gifts, fellow !   Know, I have none for thee in mine hand.

POLYDEUCES.

How, none ?—not so much as the boon of drinking at yonder spring ?

AMYCUS.

Thou shalt learn, when thy lips at noon are parched and languishing.

POLYDEUCES.

For silver, or what price, say, shall we win of thee this grace ?

AMYCUS.

Raise hands for the boxing-fray ; meet a champion face to face.

POLYDEUCES.

With fists alone, or with play of feet, eye on eye evermore ?

AMYCUS.

Let thy fists do all they may : spare not thy ring-craft's lore.

POLYDEUCES.

And who is the man who must try the weight of mine hand and my glove ?

AMYCUS.

Thou seest him—lo, he is nigh.   No maiden the boxer will prove !

POLYDEUCES.

What prize to the victor shall fall, for the which we match our might ? 70

AMYCUS.

Thou or I shall become the thrall of whoso wins this fight.

POLYDEUCES.

Out !   For such triumphs' sake fight red-combed birds !   'twere shame !

AMYCUS.

Whether as cocks we make us, or lions, 'tis one and the same
Unto me : for no other stake will we battle than such as I name.

So Amycus spake, and roared from his shell one shattering blast,
And thereat a shag-haired horde of Bebrycians gathering fast,
As the breath from the great shell poured, 'neath the shade of the plane-
    trees passed.
And, to summon the heroes, the fearless, thitherward, hasted away
Castor the battle-peerless to where Ship Argo lay.
So when in the gauntlets of stout ox-hide they had sheathed their
    hands,   80
And had deftly coiled about their arms the long lithe bands,
In the midst, with death in the blast of his breath, each champion stands.
Then with mighty endeavour the twain, all eager to close in fight,
Tried which of the two should gain the vantage of back to the light :
But by ring-craft didst thou outpace, Polydeuces, thy giant foe,
And fell upon Amycus' face the full sun's dazzling glow.
Forthright in a fury-flame of wrath rushed the giant on
Outflashing his fists : as he came, was he smitten by Tyndareus' son

On the point of the jaw : he was wrought unto fiercer rage, pain-stung.
In whirlwind fashion he fought ; his whole weight forward he flung 90
Face-downwards. Yelled to their king the Bebrycians ; the heroes
    cheered
From the farther side of the ring Polydeuces the strong ; for they feared
Lest, seeing the lists were strait, their man might haply be
Overborne by the giant's weight, for as Tityos huge was he.
But to this side and that side aye traversed Zeus' son : now with his
    right,
Now with his left would he flay the seed of Poseidon ; his might
That onset availed to stay, in his giant bulk's despite.
Now reeling 'neath blows he stood like a drunken man ; he spat
Forth of his mouth the blood, and the heroes cheered thereat,
Beholding him battered and cut—lips, jaws, one hideous wound, 100
And the eyes of him well-nigh shut as the brute-face swelled around.
Worried and flurried him then the prince on every hand
With flickering feints ; but when all 'wildered he marked him stand,
A lightning fist to the bend 'twixt eyebrow and nose he flashed :
From his forehead the flesh did it rend to the bone : by the stroke down
    dashed
On his back outstretched he lay on the earth that the green leaves strewed ;
But he sprang to his feet, and the fray was in grimmer earnest renewed.
With gauntlet-buffets hailing, each other's destruction they sought ;
But ever with blows unavailing the lord of Bebrycia fought ;
They touched but the chest, they slid by the neck ; but with blow upon
    blow 110
Zeus's invincible seed misfeatured the face of his foe.
And the sweating monster's frame was collapsing, as though in their sight
From a giant a dwarf he became, but the other's breadth and height
Waxed as he warmed to the fray ; more bright did his colour glow.
And how did he—Song-goddess, say—lay that huge glutton low ?
Speak, for thou knowest : my tongue but interprets for others : I tell
All that thou wilt, that my song may be chanted as pleaseth thee well.
    The giant's spirit was wrought up now for a mighty essay :
With his own left hand he caught Polydeuces' left, and away

From his old ward slantwise swerved, to the right made a forward
    stride,   120
And a right arm broad as a curved ship-beam swung up from his side.
Had the blow gone home, he had sped but ill, Amyclae's king ;
But beneath it he stooped his head : with a mighty right-arm swing,
By the heave of his shoulder up-driven, his foe's left temple he met.
Forth from a wound wide-riven in the temple did dark blood jet,
While his left hand flashed to his mouth, and clashed the teeth close-set.
The hail of his swift blows crashed on the face of his foe evermore,
Till now were his cheek-bones smashed : he fell, and on earth's green floor
Half-swooning he lay, and upheld, as yielding the victory,
Both hands, for utterly quelled, yea, nigh unto death was he.   130
Yet thou didst not use thy right of victor tyrannously,
Thou lord of the cestus-fight, but a mighty oath unto thee
By the name of his father he swore, of Poseidon the King of the Sea,
That to strangers never more despiteous would he be.
   Lo, Prince, I have chanted thy praise. Now, Castor, I hymn thee—
    hail,
Lord of the chariot-race, of the spear, of the brazen mail !
   Zeus' scions twain had torn from their home the daughters two
Of Leucippus, nor far had they borne them, ere hotly did twain pursue
Which were brethren, Aphareus' sons, even Lynceus and Idas the strong :
For those fair ravished ones should have been their brides ere long.   140
But at Aphareus' tomb they stayed that headlong chase and flight :
From their chariots they leapt, and arrayed them, two against two, for
    fight,
Sloping the arched shield's weight, and swinging the lance on high.
Yet through his helm with a great voice first did Lynceus cry :
" Why, caitiffs, lust ye for fight ? How lawlessly seek ye to tear
Brides from their first troth-plight, with swords in your hands made bare ?
Unto us did Leucippus betroth his daughters long before
Ye coveted them ; yea, an oath to give them to us he swore.
Unrighteously have ye wrought, who for wives of other men
Proffered oxen and mules—yea, brought wealth filched from others ere
    then,

To pervert a father thereby, and ye robbed us by bribery !
Sooth, many a time did I—of few words though I be—
Say to your faces this, yea, to thy face and thine ;
' Friends, not for your honour it is that the sons of a princely line
Should be seeking to win wives so, which have pledged unto others the
    hand.
Sure, Sparta is wide enow, and Elis the chariot-land,
And Arcadia's pastures, and where Achaia's cities stand,
And Messene, and Argos the fair, and all the Sisyphian strand.
There wait in many a home many maidens passing praise
In flawless beauty's bloom, and wise in the household's ways.   160
Whomsoever ye will ye twain of these full lightly may win,
For fathers many are fain of high-born marriage-kin,
And ye be pre-eminent amid all the hero-race,
As were your sires ; your descent is of immemorial days.
Friends, let the accomplishment of our bridals for us twain thrive,
So all with one intent will we aid you nobly to wive.'
With many such words I pleaded ; but far by the winds were they borne
Over weltering waves unheeded ; ye had naught for my prayers but scorn,
For callous and ruthless were ye.   Yet even now give ear :
Behold now, cousins are we, by our fathers' brotherhood near.   170
But if your hearts be set upon war, if our feud be a chain
That blood must dislink, that must wet the spears with the life's red
    rain,
Let Idas and mighty-souled Polydeuces his cousin refrain
Their hands from the fight, and hold them aloof from the battle-strain.
But let us at the War-god's bar plead now, even Castor and me,
For the younger-born we are : not utter misery
Let us leave to our fathers ; suffice that of one house one son fall,
So the others shall live to rejoice with bridal-festival—
Not corpses, but bridegrooms—friend and kinsman, and take to wife
These maids.   Good were it to end with small scathe mighty strife." 180
   Then—for the All-beholders would not that his words be in vain—
They cast on the earth from their shoulders their harness of war, they
    twain

Which were elder ; and Lynceus came forth into the midst of the field :
Flickered his spear-point's flame 'neath the uttermost rim of his shield ;
And before him the restless head of the lance of Castor gleamed.
From the crests of their helmets shed the dark plumes stormily streamed,
While with hardest endeavour they tried to plunge the lance-point there
Where this one or that espied for an instant the flesh laid bare.
But the spears, or ever blood of one by other was shed,
Fast-wedged in the linden-wood of the shields, brake short by the head.   190
But forth of the scabbards they tore their swords, and to compass the death
Of each other they strove once more, neither gave they the battle breath.
Oft Castor at Lynceus' wide shield thrust and his helmet-crest ;
Oft Lynceus the eagle-eyed lunged out at the fence of his breast,
Yet his sword-point did but win to the crimson plume : but at last,
When Lynceus lashed with his keen blade down at a knee shown past
The shield-rim, Castor drew that foot back, smote, and shred
His fingers away ; straight flew the sword from his hand : he fled
Thence to his father's tomb, where Idas sat in his might
And watched the decision of doom, the kindred warriors' fight.   200
Rushed on him Tyndareus' son : through his flank he plunged the blade,
Through his bowels the point cleft on, and a broad death-pathway it made
To his navel. The proud head drooped ; on the red earth Lynceus lay,
And down on his eyelids swooped sleep leaden-winged straightway.
Ah, Laocoösa their mother saw never thereafter, beside
The hearth of their sires, his brother, a bridegroom with his bride !
For Messenian Idas clenched his grip on the column up-piled
Upon Aphareus' tomb ; he wrenched it away, and with fierce haste wild
Would have swung it down on his head who had laid his brother dead—-
But Zeus averted the blow, for the carven marble he dashed   210
From his hands, and blasted the foe with his thunderbolt earthward flashed.
Thus hard were his task who would war with Tyndareus' mighty sons,
Seeing He which begat them is far the mightiest of mighty ones.

Hail, Leda's Sons ! Evermore upon this my minstrelsy
Fairest renown do ye pour ! To the Tyndarids all bards be
Dear, and to Helen, and all those Heroes that thronged to aid
Menelaus, and Troy's proud wall full low in destruction laid.
O princes, your high renown rang out from the Chian's lips,
When he chanted of Priam's town, when he sang the Achaian ships,
And the battles round Ilium fought, and Achilles, a tower of fight.   220
And to you in my turn have I brought the Muses' spells of delight
By the clear-voiced Song-queens given, yea, all mine house's best.
O, of all good gifts of Heaven is Song the loveliest !

IDYLL XXIII.

A legend of Love's Retribution.[1]

A LOVER there was : sick-souled he sighed for a scornful fair ;
Lovely she was to behold, but a loveless heart she bare.
For his love did she render hate ; no kindness to him would she show ;
And she knew not Love, how great a God he is, what a bow
He graspeth, how bitterly his arrows in young hearts quiver.
If he spake to her, yea, drew nigh, as adamant was she ever.
No assuaging there was of his flame, no smile flickered forth to meet him ;
No light in her eyes when he came, no rose in her cheek would greet him :
Not a kiss, not a word would she spare, to lighten his load thereby.
As a beast of the forest will glare on the hunters with trustless eye,   10
So evermore did she bear her to him : there was scornful hate
On her lips, and her eyes' cold stare was inexorable as fate.
In her face was the reflex borne of her mood : its rose would fade,
It was clothed with the insult of scorn, at his presence.   Yet all this made
Her yet more adorably fair : her pride but enkindled desire.
    At the last he could no more bear the Love-queen's torturing fire,
But he went and he wept upon that threshold of hate and pride,
And he kissed the lintel-stone, and he lifted his voice and cried :
" Harsh, froward all words above !   Thou lion's fosterling !
Thou marble, unworthy of love !   I come to thee now, and I bring   20
The last of my gifts, my neck's death-noose.   Nevermore for aye,
Girl, shall I anger or vex thee : nay, but I fare on the way
Whereto thou hast sentenced me, where flows by the path, as they tell,
Lorn love's one remedy, the Forgetful River of Hell.
Ah, though I should drain with my burning lips all Lethe's flood,
Not thus should I quench my yearning desire !   On thy door's cold wood
I imprint my farewell.   I foresee the fate that awaiteth thee :—

1. I have taken the same liberty with this idyll as some other translators have done,
and for the same reason—that thus a *motif* which is revolting to modern readers is con-
verted into one which can claim their sympathy.

Ah, the rose is a lovely thing, yet at time's touch fadeth away :
Fair is the violet in spring—its youth is but for a day :
White is the lily—but lo, it has drooped, and withered it lies :⠀⠀⠀30
White are the crystals of snow—they melt as they fall from the skies :
And fair is the grace of youth—in the space of an hour it dies.
The time shall come, when the dart of Love shall sting thee deep,
Even thee, when with burning heart the brine-bitter tears thou shalt weep.
Ah, fair one, do thou bestow this one last kindness on me—
When forth of thy door thou shalt go, and thy lover hanging shalt see
In thy porch, ah, pass me not by !⠀⠀One moment beside the dead
Stand weeping !⠀⠀Ah, let thine eye the libation of pity shed !
Unknit this cord, and cast thy mantle on me for a pall ;
So hide me.⠀⠀A kiss, for the last, first time, on my brow let fall :⠀⠀40
This grace of thy lips let me take in death :—O fear me not, child,
Whom not even thy kiss can awake to forgive and be reconciled !
Scoop me a grave, where my love shall be hidden away, and cry
Thrice, in departing, above me :⠀⠀" In peace, O lover, lie ! "
Say, if thou wilt, furthermore :⠀⠀" Unto death was he loyal to me."
Write, too, this legend—I score it now on thy wall for thee :—
" This man Love slew : O pass not, wayfarer, heedlessly :
But pause, and murmur, ' Alas for the loved one's cruelty ' ! "
⠀⠀⠀Then a stone did he take and bring afront of her door ; to the wall
He leaned that fearful thing, and he tied to the door-post tall⠀⠀⠀50
That slender cord of death, and the noose cast over his head :
That foot-rest he spurned from beneath him, and there was he hanging, dead !
⠀⠀⠀Forth came that maid of her door, and she saw where her lover hung
Dead over her own home's floor ; yet her heart was nowise wrung :
O'er the horror no tear she shed : she brushed by him, filing so
The robes of her maidenhead !⠀⠀To the ball-play then did she go ;
And thence did she speed her feet to a quiet pool, and here
The insulted God did she meet ; for above the water clear
On a stone slab Eros stood.⠀⠀As the girl leapt into the flood,
Leapt also the image, and killed the wicked.⠀⠀A broad blood-streak⠀⠀60
Crimsoned the water, and thrilled was the air, as upfloated a shriek :—
" Lovers, rejoice ! for see, she is slain who with hate met love !
Hearts faithful and true, love ye !⠀⠀Your avenger the God will prove."

IDYLL XXIV.

How Heracles, when a baby, strangled two serpents sent by Hera to destroy him.

Now had Heracles seen the light ten months, and Iphicles his brother
Was younger than he by a night, when Alcmena of Midea, their mother,
Bathed them, and gave of the breast their fill, and she laid them to rest
In the goodly brazen shield which Amphitryon won when he slew
Pterelaus in foughten field : there cradled lay these two,
Then, stroking each bright head, low sang she over their bed :
" Sleep, babies mine, sweet sleep !   O sleep, but to waken again !
Sleep, O my souls !   God keep you, dear little brothers twain !
Bliss be your dreams, till the dawning's beams bring bliss in their train ! "
   She rocked, while thus did she croon, the great shield, and they slept. 10
But when now at the night's mid-noon the Bear to the westward swept
Ever watching Orion upheaving his giant shoulder of flame,
Then from Hera the mischief-weaving two serpent-monsters came.
As the dark-blue coils rolled on, upbristled the scales that they bore :
O'er the broad smooth threshold-stone, 'twixt the fluted posts of the door,
She sped them, to rend with their jaws the young babe Heracles.
Trailing their ravening maws fast over the floor slid these.
As the twain came onward, out of their eyes a death-flame flashed,
And the venomous slaver about their baleful jaws was dashed.
Those flickering tongues full nigh to the boys by this had won,   20
When suddenly woke—for the eye of Zeus looked down thereon—
Alcmena's babes.   Now gleamed weird light through the chambers dim.
Straightway Iphicles screamed, when over the deep shield's rim
Uprose those shapes of dismay, and the merciless white fangs met
His eyes.   He spurned away the fleecy coverlet,
Frantic to flee.   But faced them Heracles now, and his hands
Gripped, and with fingers braced like iron's overmastering bands,

He clutched those throats wherethrough is distilled the venom-store
Of the death-drink serpents brew, which the very Gods abhor.
Round the suckling born out of due time lapped they the coils hard-
    straining   30
To crush him, whom nurse never knew to utter a cry of plaining.
Then limp were they hanging again, with spires outwearied, that found
No way of escape from the chain of doom that gripped them round.
  But it pierced Alcmena's ear, that cry ; and she woke, and she said :
" Amphitryon, up ! cold fear hath seized me, and shrinking dread.
Up !   Oh tarry not to tie thy sandal-latchet thou !
Dost hear not how wild a cry from our younger-born ringeth now ?
Dost mark not—albeit 'tis dead of night—how the walls are gleaming
All round, as though overshed with the splendour of dawn's eyes beaming ?
I know there is some strange thing in the house—there is, dear lord ! " 40
  Straightway from the couch did he spring to the floor at her instant
    word :
He caught at the battle-brand keen, of the carven hilt, that was slung
Evermore from a brazen pin, o'er the cedarn bed's head hung ;
And now at the baldric-band new-plaited thereof he caught,
While grasped in his other hand was the scabbard of lotus-wood wrought—
When suddenly plunged was the wide bed-chamber in darkness deep !
Then to his servants he cried, where they breathed long breath of sleep :
" Lights !—haste, take brands where glows the fire on the red hearth-
    floor,
My thralls ! "—back drave he with blows the massy bolts of the door.
" Up, thralls stout-hearted, give ear !   Lo, the master it is doth call ! " 50
Cried a Syrian maid, as she leapt from the millstone whereby she slept.
Straightway the men drew near, with blazing brands came all,
All hasting because of fear in the night, and thronged was the hall.
They saw by the flare of the brands young Heracles : monsters twain
That suckling's soft babe-hands yet gripped as they hung there slain ;
And in panic amaze did they cry : but unto his father he
Held up the serpents, and high did he leap in his childish glee,
And his mouth with laughter was filled, at his father's feet as he cast
Those terrible monsters, stilled in the sleep of death at last.

Then did Alcmena lay on her bosom Iphicles' head :
Bloodless he was with dismay, and he quivered in frenzy of dread.   60
But over his brother the fleece of a lamb Amphitryon spread,
And he turned him again to the peace and slumber of his own bed.

   As the cocks' third call rang clear to the first faint flush of the day,
Alcmena sent for the seer Teiresias, who wont to say
Truth only : of what befell in the night she told him all,
And she prayed him to answer and tell what issue thereof should befall—
" And if haply the Gods have thought to devise for us evil herein,
In compassion to me hide it not : the doom that Fate doth spin
On swift-flashing threads, may none escape, for certain it is.
O prophet Eueres' son, what need that I teach thee this ? "   70
   So did she speak : and the seer made answer, boding good :
" O mother of heroes, fear not, daughter of Perseus' blood !
Fear not : in thine heart lay fair store up of blessings to be.
By mine eyes' dear light do I swear, which long since fled from me :
Many women Achaian that twine the yarn about the knee,
As their fingers smooth it fine, shall at evenfall sing of thee,
Shall chant Alcmena's fame : thee daughters of Greece shall revere,
So mighty a man this same thy son to the star-studded sphere
Is destined at last to soar : broad-breasted hero, all
Fierce beasts of the field before him, all mightiest men, shall fall.   80
Twelve Labours fulfilled, he is fated to dwell with Zeus in his heaven ;
But all of him mortal created to Trachis' pyre shall be given.
And the Queen of Olympus shall name him her kinsman, she at whose hest
From their den those monsters came to rend the babe at the breast.
Yea, and the day shall dawn when the jag-toothed wolf, though he find
In his lair the tender fawn, to harm her shall have no mind.
But, lady, have ready beneath the ashes the red-glowing fire,
And prepare thou faggots of heath for the burning, or faggots of brier,
Or of thorn, or of wild-pear dry and tempest-buffeted.
On the billets rough piled high burn yon two serpents dread   90
At the midnight hour, when they sought to devour thy babe in his bed.
At the dawning let one of thine handmaids gather the ashes grey ;
On the river-bank let her stand, and fling all far away

H

From the ragged rock, without thy borders, and so return
Looking not back. Throughout thine house then first do thou burn
Pure sulphur ; with water blent with salt, as the rite doth command,
From a filleted bough besprent be the floor on every hand.
And to Zeus who sitteth on high do thou sacrifice a boar,
That yours may be victory over all your foes evermore."
   He spake, and his ivory chair thrust back, and was gone : the tread   100
Of the seer was of one who bare no burden of years on his head.
   At the knee of his mother grew, like sapling in orchard grown,
Heracles. All men knew him for son of Amphitryon.
By an ancient mighty one were letters taught to the lad,
Even Linus, Apollo's son ; and a sleepless guardian he had.
And to strain the bow, and to wing the shaft with unerring hands,
Eurytus taught him, a king of wide ancestral lands.
Of Eumolpus learned he song, yea, the son of Philammon taught
His fingers to wander along the lyre of boxwood wrought.
All turns and twists of hip and of foot, whereby the fall   110
Is given by wrestlers who trip and throw in Argos, and all
Ring-craft of the cestus-fight, all serpentine writhings found
Where cunning and bodily might strive out their strife on the ground,
Such lore of the athlete-war did he learn from Phanotê's king
Harpalycus : none that from far beheld him stand in the ring,
Were he never so hardy, would dare his fist or his grip to abide,
So grim was the lion-glare of the stern face lowering-eyed.
   And to drive the chariot-steed, and the very goal to shave,
Yet in wheeling with whirlwind speed to keep unscratched the nave,
Amphitryon's own self trained herein of his love his son,   120
For treasured guerdons, gained by the swift car, oft had he won
In Argos the horse-fed land. Unshattered still and strong
Were his chariots, and naught but the hand of time had marred one thong.
   And to thrust with the spear, but to hide the shoulder well with the ward
Of the shield, and unflinching to bide the devouring edge of the sword,
And to order the ranks, with the eye to measure the strength of a band
Of the foe, as their line draweth nigh, and the squadrons of horse to com-
    mand,

Castor the good knight taught, who from Argos outlawed came
When her vine-lands wide were brought 'neath Tydeus' sway ; for the
    same
Had Adrastus bequeathed him, the meads of Argos the land of steeds. 130
Mid the demigods all, in the lore of battle, was none, of a truth,
Like Castor, till old age wore down slowly the strength of his youth.
    So did Alcmena win wise teachers and leal for the boy.
And hard by his father's bed was the couch of Heracles spread,
A lion's fell, and therein he joyed with a hero's joy.
On roast flesh ever he dined, with a mighty Dorian cake
In a maund—a delving hind long fast therewith might break.
But a supper by no fire dressed and meagre enow took he,
And his simple unbroidered vest fell scantly below his knee.

IDYLL XXV.

*Heracles visits the great farm-stead of Augeias, king of Elis, and there tells
the story of his slaying of the Nemean Lion.*

SPAKE the warder of fruits of the soil, the delver of orchard-lands—
And therewith did he cease from the toil that lay between his hands :
" Whereof thou dost inquire will I tell to thee everything,
For I fear the terrible ire of Hermes the Highway-king ;
For of all the Abiders on High he chiefly is wroth, men say,
If one in his need deny the stranger who asketh the way.
 The flocks of Augeias feed, his fair-fleeced sheep shall be found
In no one pasture-mead, on no one grazing-ground ;
But there be that crop the grass on the banks of Elisus that grows,
Through the hallowed fields some pass where Alpheius the holy flows : 10
Where Buprasium's vineyards are, some wander, and some hereby :
So likewise the folds of them far from each other sundered lie.
But, though ever his cattle increase in measure overflowing,
Here all their pasture-leas spread, ever with grass lush-growing
By Menius' watermeads wide, for the dewy meadows stand
Thick upon every side with sweet grass : all the land
Is clothed with fatness ; the might so waxeth of hornèd kine.
And there, away to thy right, their steadings, an endless line,
Stretch, even the byres of them all, beyond the river's flow,
There where the plane-trees tall in dense battalions grow,   20
And the green wild-olives that cover the temple-precinct fair
Of Apollo the pasture-lover, who heareth and answereth prayer.
Long rows of huts hard by be built for the hinds of our lord,
For us which loyally evermore keep watch and ward
O'er the measureless wealth of our king, as over the deep-furrowed field
Thrice, four times ploughed, we fling the hope of the harvest's yield.

Only his vine-dressers know the borders of all, I wot,
Which unto his wine-fats go, hard-toiling when summer is hot.
For all this far-stretching plain doth to gracious Augeias belong,
Yon fields of golden grain, yon garths where the fruit-trees throng,   30
To the border-ridge of the mountain that flasheth with many a fountain.
Here day after day and all day long in toil be passed
By us, as is meet for the thrall whose lot mid the acres is cast.
 Yet in any wise tell to me now—and profit to thee shall it bring—
In quest of whom comest thou thus hitherward journeying ?
Art thou seeking Augeias my lord ?   Or shall it be haply a thrall
Of the host that obey his word ?   I will tell to thee surely all,
What thing soever I know ; for not of a base-born line
A scion thou art, nor, I trow, base showeth that presence of thine,
So stately thou art to see.   The Heroes of heavenly birth   40
Must surely be like unto thee, when they stand mid the sons of earth ! "
 And Zeus' strong son to the old man straight spake answering :
" Yea, ancient, I would behold Augeias, even the king
Of Epeians : I seek unto him to speak of a needful thing.
If then in the city, where gather his people, now he abides,
And cares for his folk as a father, and judgments and causes decides,
Point out, old man, to me here, yea, lead me where I shall find
Some worshipful overseer of the labour of herdman and hind
Unto whom I may tell my want, and may hearken his counsel then :
For in all men the Gods implant this need of their brother men."   50
 Unto him that ancient replied, the godlike lord of the plough :
" Stranger, some God was the guide that led thee hitherward now ;
For thine heart's desire straightway no sooner is uttered than won.
Lo, Augeias my lord this day, the Sun-god's own dear son,
Is here with his son in place, with the might of Phyleus' pride.
Yestreen after many days hitherward from the city he hied
On his countless possessions to gaze, which fill the countryside.
For in kings' hearts also, I wis, doth this persuasion lie
That no such warder there is of the house as the master's eye.
Nay, come, let us hasten to where he is : lo, thee will I bring   60
To the place of our dwellings, and there thyself shalt behold the king."

Then led he on ; but within him his heart was marvelling sore—
As he marked the lion's skin, and the club that the hero bore—
Whence might the stranger have come, and fain had he asked him the
    same ;
But fear evermore struck dumb the word to his lips as it came,
Lest out of season to one that in haste thus onward sped
He should speak—forasmuch as by none is the heart of his neighbour read.
    Now the dogs, as nearer they drew, from afar of their coming were
    ware :
By the footfall-beat they knew, by the scent of flesh on the air ;
And from this side and that with wild and clamorous barking they ran 70
At the Hero, Amphitryon's child ; but about that grey-haired man
Aimlessly leaping they bayed a welcome, and fawned around :
But the old hind stooped, and made as to catch up stones from the ground,
And scared them from Heracles, and with harsh and threatening shout
He chid them, and caused to cease from their yelping the furious rout.
Yet glad was his heart that aye they watched o'er the house of their lord
When himself was far away, and he answered and spake the word :
" Lo now, how strangely mated with man may a beast be, as this
Which the Gods our kings have created for man !   How watchful he is !
If in like measure wit to discern had been given to his vigilant brain,   80
And he knew against whom he should turn his wrath, and from whom to
    refrain,
There had been no creature on earth that could rival this in worth :
But zeal uncontrolled and furious-souled is zealous in vain."
    So spake he, and onward they pressed, and therewith to his dwelling
    they came.
And by this the sun to the west had turned his steeds of flame
On-leading the gloaming-tide ; and the fat sheep even then
Trooped home from the pastures wide, and streamed into fold and pen.
And next thereafter kine unnumbered in crowds on crowds
On-coming were seen, as line upon line of rain-laden clouds
Go drifting across the heaven in forward-hurrying race   90
By the might of the south-wind driven, or the north that bloweth from
    Thrace.

No man may tell their tale as on through the welkin they sail
Unresting : by strength of the wind such hosts roll onward fast
In the vanguard, and ever behind them are fresh battalions massed ;
So herds upon herds unending of the cattle were onward wending.
Crowded were pathway and road, and hidden was all the plain,
As the living flood still flowed : too strait were the fields to contain
Their lowing ; and byre and stall with the kine of the shambling tramp
Filled fast, and the folds with all those white sheep seemed like a camp.

Then, of those thralls untold, untoiling was found not one   100
That stood by byre or fold, as a man that work had none ;
But this to a milker stooped, and her restive feet made fast
With the milking-clog, safe-looped with the thongs that around them he
    cast :
And by that was the dear calf, fain of the loving mother's teat,
Set 'neath the udder, to drain therefrom milk warm and sweet.
A pail one held, and the curd of the creamy cheese one pressed,
While another was penning the herd of the bulls apart from the rest.
And Augeias marked, as he strode from steading to steading there,
How shepherd and neatherd bestowed on their lord's wealth sleepless care.
And his son, and Heracles' might aye deeply pondering,   110
Went with him, through infinite possessions as passed the king.

And, though no trouble might break the iron-tempered mood
Of Amphitryon's son, nor shake that soul on the rock that stood,
Yet in 'wildered amaze he stared at the host past numbering
Of the cattle : no mortal had dared to say, nor had dreamed such thing,
That one man could have possessed such riches, no, nor ten,
Though in flocks they were wealthiest of all the kings of men.
To his son did Helios give this boon transcending all,
To be chiefest of all that live in the wealth of fold and stall.
So the Sun-god gave increase evermore, yea, unto the end,   120
Of his herds, nor did any disease on his cattle-steadings descend :
Yea, from all that may spoil the herdman's toil did he shield and defend
Those kine, and they multiplied fast, and ever they waxed more fair
As the years of plenty passed, and fruitful ever they were :
No calves untimely were cast, and females chiefly they bare.

And bulls three hundred went companioning these evermore,
White-shanked, and with horns bow-bent ; and others there were, ten-
score,
Red-coated, and all full-grown, of age with the kine to mate.
But beside these, herded alone, to the Sun-god consecrate
Were twelve bulls : white were they ; each one as a radiant swan   130
Gleamed ; amid all the array of the trail-foot kine they shone ;
And, as holding the rest in scorn, on the lush grass fed they apart,
And as princes royally-born they bare them in pride of their heart.
And whene'er from the tangled brake to the plain swift beasts of prey
Came stealing down to take what kine soever might stray,
These foremost to fight ever passed : for the scent of the spoilers straight
Charged they, with death in the blast of their breath and their eyes' dark
hate.
    But all were in strength outdone and in reckless arrogance far
By the mighty Phaethon, who was likened unto a star   [140
By the herdmen, for, pacing on through the thronging kine, mid the rest
Clear-seen as a star he shone that flasheth on Night's dark breast.
The sun-dried fell of the lion, the flame-faced beast, he spied,
And he charged on Amphitryon's scion, who watched him the while keen-
eyed,
Fierce-eager to shock with his brow of rock the hero's side.
But as down on the hero he dashed, his brawny hand outflashed :
On the beast's left horn he clenched his grip, and down to the dust
That massive neck he wrenched : with his shoulder's mighty thrust
Backward the bull he flung, while the corded muscles, round
The sinews tensely strung, on his arm made a living mound.
And the king and his son at the sight were astonied ; amazed at the
deed   150
Was every herdman-wight who tended the kine on the mead,
When they saw the resistless might of Zeus' and Amphitryon's seed.
    Now a little thereafter the twain, even Phyleus and Heracles,
Citywards fared from the plain of the herds and the deep-grassed leas.
But even as these 'gan tread the highway, whose feet in haste
Hitherto on a pathway had sped that was narrow and faintly traced—

For it stretched from the steadings away through the vineyards, and,
    over-grassed,
Dim in the shadows it lay with green boughs overcast—
Then the son of Augeias said to the scion of Zeus most high—
For ever, as onward he led, the hero followed nigh—   160
Rightward turning his head o'er his shoulder courteously :
" Stranger, awhile agone was a story told unto me ;
And now, as I muse thereon, methinks it concerneth thee :
A wayfaring man—by his frame, in the noontide of life—from the land
Of Argolis hitherward came, an Achaian from Helikê's strand ;
And a tale to our ears he bare, which Epeians heard not a few,
How, when himself was there, a certain Argive slew
A monster, a lion, the fear of the fields and the curse thereof,
Whose cavern-lair was near Zeus' holy Nemean grove.
I cannot certainly tell if from Argos the slayer had come,   170
Or in Tiryns wont to dwell, or had in Mycenae his home.
Even such was the tale that he told, and the mighty hunter withal
Was sprung from Perseus of old, if rightly his word I recall.
I trow, no Argive beside could have dared and done this thing
Save thee ; and the lion's hide is silently witnessing
To a deed by thy strong hands done, as it resteth against thy side.
Come now, first answer me one thing ; let me be certified
If I rightly divine of thee herein, O hero, or not :—
Say, art thou verily he whose deed to our ears he brought,
The Achaian from Helikê, and true touching thee was my thought ? 180
Say, how didst thou slay yon pest of destruction, with none to aid ?
How came it thus to infest that Nemean river-glade ?
For in Apian land shall be found nowhere such a monstrous curse,
Though of purpose thou search her round : no beast so huge doth she nurse,
But the bear, and the forest-boar, and the wolf, the pest of the fold,
And for this cause marvelled the more those hearing the story told ;
And there were that cried mid the throng that he spake a lying word,
With the talk of an idle tongue to pleasure them that heard."
   Therewith did the prince give place from the midst of the highway wide,
That so might be left clear space for the hero to draw to his side, 190

That the better so might he hear the speech of Heracles.
So came the hero near, and he spake, and his words were these :
" Touching that which first thou hast sought, O son of Augeias, to learn,
As a plummet true is thy thought, and lightly dost thou discern.
So of this weird monster-thing the tale unto thee will I tell
For the which thou art hungering, and how his slaying befell.
But I tell not how came he there : though many the Argives be,
None of them all can declare that mystery certainly.
Only we guessed that a God for neglected sacrifice broke
Into anger, and laid this rod of his wrath on Phoroneus' folk.   200
On the folk of the low-lying land like a storm-swollen river he burst,
Slew, ravaged on every hand, and Bembina's people the worst ;
Unendurable things they bare, for their village was nigh to his lair.
Of the toils that were laid on thy guest by Eurystheus was this the first,
For he spake unto me his behest to slay this monster accurst.
So I took my supple bow, and my quiver arrow-fraught,
And forth on the quest did I go, with the club in my right hand caught,
The mace without a flaw, a wild-olive stem unstripped,
Green wood, the which I saw upon Helicon's side, and gripped,
And forth of its bed with its roots wide-spread that trunk I ripped.   210
    When I came to the thicket-cover wherein that lion was hid,
I grasped my bow, and over the curved horn-tip I slid
The plaited string, and the notch of the arrow I fitted thereto.
For the fell brute then did I watch ; all round me my glance I threw,
If him I might haply espy ere his glance had his hunter descried.
And by this was the sun noon-high, but no footprint had I spied
Telling where he had passed before, and I hearkened in vain for his roar.
No man appeared to me there that with oxen bent to his task,
Through the furrows driving the share for the sowing, of whom I might
        ask ;
Nay, all to their steadings had fled, and their jailor was pallid dread.   220
Yet I refrained not my feet from questing the leaf-shadowed height
Of the mountain, until I should meet him, and match with his my might.
    Suddenly there he stood : as the even drew nigh, to his lair,
Full-gorged with flesh and with blood, he paced : gore dabbled the hair

Of his sun-parched mane, and clung red gouts 'neath his fierce bright eyes
And his chest : o'er his jaws his tongue rolled, flickering serpent-wise.
Then crouched I down in the shade of a thicket, hid from his eye
On the edge of the hill-forest glade, and awaited his drawing nigh.
Then shot I at his left flank, and smote it, as nearer he drew,
But in vain, for nowise sank the keen shaft-head therethrough,   230
But back from his hide did it leap to the green grass, bootlessly sped.
Swift up from the ground did he sweep the mane of his tawny head
In amaze : he glared about him, with fierce eyes seeking his foe :
From his cavernous jaws gleamed out white fangs in a murderous row.
Once more my bow I drew, and an arrow again I shot,
Sore vexed that the first shaft flew from mine hands at the beast for
     naught.
To his mid-chest fair did it win, where run the channels of breath,
Yet pierced not then through his skin the arrow of anguished death,
But it fell at his feet, as vain as a breath of the idle wind.
For the third time I set me again to draw, sore chafed in my mind.   240
But now, as around him flashed his eyes, his foe had he spied,
And the terrible monster lashed with his long tail either side.
Forthwith was he hot for the fight : a thundercloud of ire
Was his neck ; stood his mane upright like tongues of raging fire.
His curving spine was bent like the arch of a straining bow :
Under loins and flanks was his pent-up fury of strength gathered now.
And even as a chariot-wright, at manifold crafts right good,
Bends saplings, shapen aright with the knife, of the wild fig's wood,
When first by the fire he hath dried them, to fashion him tyres for his
     car :   [250
As he archeth the lithe stem round, from his grasp doth it suddenly bound,
And with one leap slipping aside from his hands hath it flown afar ;
So the terrible lion, power and fury together massed,
Leapt on me, mad to devour my flesh : my left hand cast
Before me my thick cloak, flung round mine arrows, to shield my face,
The while my right hand swung o'er mine head the storm-toughened mace.
Down on his brow I dashed it, and, full on the shaggy crown
Of the murderous monster as crashed the knotted olive-wood down,

It was snapped in twain : from the air to the earth, ere his leap reached
    me,
Down had he fallen, and there upon trembling feet stood he,
And his head to and fro he rocked, for rushed o'er the fierce eyes twain 260
Darkness, so shaken and shocked by the blow in his skull was the brain.
Then, when I marked him distraught with overmastering pain,
Ere he could turn him, or caught his breath unto him again,
My bow to the earth had I cast, and my quiver broidery-decked,
Unwares had I leapt on him, fast had I clutched him, the iron-necked,
And choked him in that stern grip ; from behind were my hard hands
    strangling
The monster, lest he should rip my limbs with claws red-mangling.
On his hind feet heavily tramped I, crushing them down on the ground
With mine heels, while I held fast clamped his sides, with my thighs grip-
    ped round,
Till limply his forearms hung, and upright strangled he stood   270
In mine arms, and to Hades was flung the soul of its monster-brood.
Then cast I about to attain a device whereby to flay
The shaggy hide of the slain wild beast from his limbs away,—
A task exceeding hard ; for the edge of the steel it withstood,
And to cleave it I tried flint-shard all vainly, and pointed wood.[1]
Then—sure an Immortal was cause of the thought mine heart within—
" With the lion's own sharp claws will I rend asunder his skin ! "
Swiftly with these I flayed it : therein for a mantle then
And for armour, my limbs I arrayed against battle, the wounder of men.
Thus it befell that at last the Nemean Lion was slain   280
Who had wrought in the days overpast unto flocks and men much bane.

---

    1. Some critics have objected to the reading " wood " as absurd ; but Heracles per-
ceived that it was a question of counteracting *magic*, and so tried materials used in
primitive and mystic rites, flint, pointed wood, and finally horn.

MEGARA.

The authorship of this dialogue between Megara, the wife, and Alcmena the mother, of Heracles, is uncertain. Internal evidence has inclined many scholars to ascribe it to Theocritus : it is therefore placed where, if genuine, it would naturally stand as one of a series.

" My mother, why is thine heart thus stricken sorely to-day
With sorrow's bitterest dart, and the rose hath faded away
From thy cheek ?   What affliction's smart disquieteth thee ?—ah say !
Dost thou grieve for the manifold woe by thy glorious son undergone
At the hands of a caitiff foe, as a lion were thrall to a fawn ?
Ah me, that the Deathless in Heaven should have brought me to this
    estate !
Why have my parents given me birth for so evil fate ?
O hapless I, who was bride to a hero worthy to be
Evermore my glory, my pride, the very eyes of me !
With worship and honour sweet my soul bowed down at his feet ;   10
Yet none is so evil-starred of all men living as he,
None who is smitten so hard of the scourge of calamity.
Ah wretch ! with the very bow that Apollo had given to him—
Nay, some Death-spirit, I trow, or a Blood-avenger grim—
His own dear children he slew, their precious lives he spilled
In madness raving through his home, till with blood it was filled !
O misery !   I, their mother, with mine own eyes saw them shot
By their father to death !   None other, not in dreams, hath known such
    lot !
Oh their cry to their mother, the cry " Help, help us ! " till failed their
    breath !—
Naught could I do, so nigh was the irresistible death.   20
As a bird screams over her dying nestlings, ruthlessly torn

From the nest by a horrible snake, and the helpless fledgling things
In the heart of the tangled brake he devours, while her fluttering wings
Hover round, and with anguished crying wild and high doth she mourn,
But cannot avail to aid her young, neither dares draw nigh,
Being most exceeding afraid of that coiling cruelty ;
So, wretched in motherhood, through all that desolate home
Wailing for my lost brood with frenzied feet did I roam.
O Artemis, thou who art queen over womankind in thy power,
Would that I with my babes might have been laid dead in the selfsame
   hour,   30
That the arrow envenomed and keen the life of mine heart might devour !
Then had my parents, heaping with loving hands one pyre,
Laid us thereon with weeping, and cast rich gifts on the fire.
In a golden vase inurning our bones, had they laid in the earth
Those ashes grey of our burning, in the land where our race had birth.
But they dwell in Thebes' strong hold, the nurse of the war-steed, now,
And the deep Aonian mould of a far-off plain do they plough ;
But in Tiryns, the crag-built city of Hera the Queen, must I
My life long—oh, the pity of it !—must daily die
Heart-broken with grief, nor end nor relief to my tears draweth nigh. 40
 But a short, short time in our hall do mine eyes my lord behold ;
For the never-ceasing call unto labours manifold
Still waits him, by land and by sea stern labours and wanderings long—
O, a heart of rock bears he, a spirit as iron strong
In his breast. But thou, thou art poured like water out, aye weeping
All nights, all days that our Lord Zeus hath in eternal keeping.
None other there is of all my kinsfolk to stand by my side
And cheer me ; for no mere wall of a house doth the loving divide
From the loving : beyond the tall pine-woods of the Isthmus abide
All friends ; there is none unto whom I may look for sympathy—   50
A woman of darkest doom—and refresh mine heart thereby,
Save Pyrrha my sister alone ; but her trembling agonies
Of soul are yet more than mine own, in her fear for Iphicles
Thy son—for thou to a God and a man hast brought to birth
Sons bowed 'neath affliction's load beyond all children of earth."

So did she speak, and rolled tears hotter and hotter aye
Down on the vesture-fold on her lovely bosom that lay,
As of children and parents dear was the sad remembrance renewed.
And Alcmena with many a tear her pallid cheeks bedewed,
And heavily she sighed, from the depths of her heart did she moan,   60
And with earnest words she replied to the wife of her well-loved son :
" O child, my child, what thronging thoughts have thrilled thee with pain ?
Ah, why this sudden longing to torture the hearts of twain
With the unforgotten woes full oft ere this bewailed ?
Suffice they not us, all those that from birth to this day have assailed
Thee and me ? Under sorrow's spell must that man surely lie
Who could harden his heart to tell all woes we have known, thou and I !
All these which have lighted on us by the doom of the Gods have been given.
Dear child, I behold thee thus by affliction tempest-driven,
Affliction unceasing : nor I can blame thee, if overpast   70
Be thy patience—even of joy men weary and sicken at last.
Thy woes from the depths of mine heart I bemoan and compassionate
Who hast had to the full thy part in our house's evil fate,
Whereof the dread ever hangs overhead, a crushing weight.
Let the Maid and Demeter the fair-robed Queen mine heart's truth know—
Whosoever shall falsely swear by these is his own worst foe :—
I love thee mine heart within no less than if thou hadst lain
Under my girdle, hadst been the fruit of my travail-pain,
Hadst been my darling, mine own little maiden, the light of mine hall :
Yea, this, I trow, hath been known long time unto thee withal.   80
Then say not thou, O flower of my breast, that I care not for thee,
Though Niobe beautiful-tressed wept never so ceaselessly.
No man can have indignation that long should a mother lament
For her son in his tribulation. Ten months I heavily went
Ere I looked on his face, as I bore my baby mine heart beneath.
Yea, he brought me nigh to the door that is kept by the Warder of Death ;
Such birth-pangs passing-sore I endured in that travail-tide.
And now on an alien shore is he far, O far from my side
Accomplishing some new toil, and I know not, in this my woe,
If again on his fatherland-soil I shall welcome him home, or no.   90

Moreover, appalled have I been by a terrible dream in the hour
Of slumber, a vision seen of some malignant power ;
And I fear exceedingly lest harm on my two sons light.
There appeared in my dream unto me my son, even Heracles' might ;
And in both his hands did he wield a mattock massy and strong.
On the verge of a fruitful field was he delving deep and long
A trench, with strenuous stroke, like a hind that for hire works fast :
His belted tunic and cloak on the earth behind him were cast.
But when to the end of all his toil at the last he had won,
And his labour at trench and wall for the vineyard-close was done,   100
He was even at point to lean against the dyke his spade,
And to don the raiment wherein he was theretofore arrayed,
When suddenly blazed o'er the trench by his hands delved deep in the
      ground
A fire no man could quench, and the weird flame wrapped him round.
But backward ever with light-leaping feet did the hero spring
To avoid the deadly might of the rage of the dread Fire-king ;
And before his body he swung the spade, as a shield it had been,
And to right and to left he flung his glances quick and keen,
Aye watching the ravening flame, that it might not blast him and sear.
Then for his helping came great-hearted Iphicles near ;   110
But he slipped, as it seemed unto me, and heavily fell on the plain
Ere he reached him, and helplessly he lay there, and strove in vain
To rise to his feet again, like an old man strengthless all
Whom joyless eld doth constrain, how loth soever, to fall,
And there on the earth must he lie, too feeble to rise and stand,
Till haply a passer-by shall raise him up by the hand,
With old-time reverence filled for eld's beard silver-grey ;
So Iphicles, mighty to wield the buckler, in dust low lay.
And aye did I weep and weep, beholding the desperate plight
Of my sons, till my heavy sleep at the last from mine eyes took flight, 120
And with sudden blaze came the morning rays, and with radiant light.
Such ill dreams came to appal my soul through the night's long gloom,
Belovèd :—O, may they all be turned to Eurystheus' doom,
And away from our house !   May my soul be seer of vengeance sent
Upon him !   May Heaven's control none otherwise shape the event ! "

IDYLL XXVI.

How Pentheus, king of Thebes, was torn to pieces by Bacchanals.

INO and Autonoe, and Agave of cheeks apple-red,
Three bands to the hills they three in Maenad frenzy led.
These stripped the oak's rough screen of wilding leaves, and those
The ivy's living green, and the asphodel earth's lap knows.
They reared in a forest-glade twelve altars, three and nine ;
For Semele three they made, thrice three for the Lord of the Vine.
The sacred cakes did they draw from the consecrated chest,
And laid them in silent awe on the altars with green boughs dressed,
After the Wine-god's law, and in fashion as pleaseth him best,
The while from a sheer crag's height on all this Pentheus spied   10
In a lentisk hidden from sight, which grew on the mountain side.
Autonoe first discerned him : up sprang she with terrible cries ;
Her wild feet scattered and spurned the Mad God's mysteries—
Which none profane may behold,—as she leapt on them where they lay ;
For herself was frenzied-souled, and mad were the rest straightway.
Pentheus in panic fled, and they chased him furiously
With their skirts at the girdle-stead up-kilted above the knee.
" What would ye, O women ? " cried King Pentheus, as fast they drew
      near.
Autonoe fiercely replied : " Thou shalt soon know—yea, ere thou hear ! "
At his head his mother tore with a yell not human ; the cry   20
Was a lioness's roar when her cubs beside her lie.
And Ino planted her foot on his waist ; with the shoulder-blade
She rent out his arm by the root ; like part Autonoe played ;
And the remnants of that poor frame did the others piecemeal tear.
So back unto Thebes they came : all blood-bedabbled they were :
No Pentheus for mountain-game, but anguished repentance they bare

I pity him not—let no man compassionate such as rebel
Against Dionysus, though one endure things direr to tell !
Let him humble himself, and abase his pride as a child herein.
Pure may I be, and the praise of the pure in heart may I win.　　30
From the Aegis-lord of the Skies this doom shall be honoured of all :
" The seed of the righteous shall rise, the house of the wicked shall fall."
All hail, Dionysus, whom on Dracanus' snow-veiled height
Zeus the Most High from the womb of his thigh brought forth to the light !
Unto loveliest Semele hail, and her sisters the Maids Cadmeian,
Heroines ! Myriads shall fail not to chant their glory-paean
By whom this deed was done as the Wine-god wrought upon them !
Let no man blame them, let none the works of the Gods condemn.

IDYLL XXVII.

A dramatic sketch, describing a primitive wooing and wedding among Sicilian herdfolk.

MAIDEN.

A NEAT-HERD was Paris like thee, and from home stole Helen the wise.

DAPHNIS.

'Tis a Helen that now kisses me, for the favour I find in her eyes.

MAIDEN.

Boast not, rude man !   A kiss is but emptiness, so folk say.

DAPHNIS.

Yet in empty kisses there is a dear delight alway.

MAIDEN.

I wash my lips therefrom, and thy kiss, I blow it to air.

DAPHNIS.

Dost thou wash thy lips ?   Ah come, let me kiss thee again, my fair !

MAIDEN.

To be kissing thy kine will beseem thee, not touching a maid such as I.

DAPHNIS.

Boast not !—thy youth, like a dream, is swiftly fleeting by.

MAIDEN.

Raisins the cluster will be ; dried roses not utterly fail.

DAPHNIS.

Come 'neath the olives with me, that there I may tell thee a tale.   10

MAIDEN.

I will not : ere to-day has thy sweet tale proved but a cheat.

DAPHNIS.

'Neath the elms come hither away, and list to my piping sweet.

MAIDEN.

Pipe for thine own joy, clown !   No love-lorn sighings for me !

DAPHNIS.

O hush, girl !   Draw not down Aphrodite's wrath upon thee !

MAIDEN.

I will none of the Paphian ; bright be Artemis' face to me yet !

DAPHNIS.

Ah, talk not so, lest she smite thee, and tangle thee fast in her net !

MAIDEN.

Let her smite as she will !   I shall lack not the help of Artemis.

DAPHNIS.

Why doth thine hand thrust me back ?   I would but sip one kiss.

MAIDEN.

Lay not thine hand on me !—lo, if thou dost, will I tear thy lip !

DAPHNIS.

Thou canst not escape Love—no, never maiden hath given him the slip. 20

MAIDEN.

I escape him—by Pan, do I so !   Thou bearest his yoke for aye.

DAPHNIS.

I dread lest thee he bestow on a meaner man one day.

MAIDEN.

To woo me many were fain, but none to mine heart was dear.

DAPHNIS.

I of them all remain thy one true lover here.

MAIDEN.

O dear one, what can I do ?—for marriage is full of annoy.

DAPHNIS.

It hath naught to lament nor to rue, but the dancing feet of joy.

MAIDEN.

Ah no, but women, they say, at the frown of their lords are dismayed.

DAPHNIS.

Nay, over them still rule they—of whom be women afraid ?

MAIDEN.

Travail I dread : the dart of Eileithyia is keen.

DAPHNIS.

Nay—who is the queen of thy heart but Artemis, Travail-queen ?   30

MAIDEN.

Of child-bearing stand I in dread, lest my fresh bloom fade away.

DAPHNIS.

Dear sons shall crown thine head with a splendour of new-born day.

MAIDEN.

What meet bride-price shall be mine, if I lay in thine my hand ?

DAPHNIS.

All, all my flock shall be thine, my glades, and my pasture-land.

MAIDEN.

Swear—when I am won, swear now that thou never wilt leave me forlorn !

DAPHNIS.

Never !   By Pan, though thou from thy side wouldst chase me in scorn !

MAIDEN.

A home dost thou build me, and rearest thou bowers, and folds for sheep ?

DAPHNIS.

I rear for thee bowers, heart's dearest : thine are the flocks that I keep.

MAIDEN.

What tale, ah what, shall I tell to my father, the grey and old ?

DAPHNIS.

He will say this marriage was well, so soon as my name is told.   40

MAIDEN.

That name, then, of thine declare : ofttimes there is charm in a name.

DAPHNIS.

Daphnis : Nomaia bare me ; of Lycidas' loins I came.

MAIDEN.

Of gentle blood—yet mine is of no less high degree.

DAPHNIS.

O yea, fair lineage is thine, for Menalcas fathered thee.

MAIDEN.

Show me thy woodland-glade, where standeth thy cattle-stall.

DAPHNIS.

See here, how in greenness arrayed are my cypresses slender and tall.

MAIDEN.

Feed on, my goats, for I go on the neat-herd's labours to gaze.

DAPHNIS.

My bulls, to my sweet while I show my wood-lawns, peacefully graze.

MAIDEN.

Touching my breast, rude groom !—what is this thou art minded to do ?

DAPHNIS.

These first-ripe apples bloom all mellow ; I'll prove it true.   50

MAIDEN.

By Pan, I am swooning !   Take thine hand away from my side !

DAPHNIS.

Fear not, sweet love !   Why quake at thy lover, O coward bride ?

MAIDEN.

By the watercourse down hast thou drawn me, art soiling my raiment fair !

DAPHNIS.

Nay, 'neath thy cloak have I strawn this soft fleece—see, it is there.

MAIDEN.

Out upon thee !   Thou hast rent my girdle—wherefore this ?

DAPHNIS.

This for a gift I present to the Paphian : her first it is.

MAIDEN.

Stay, wretch !—sure, one draweth near unto us !—I hear a sound !

DAPHNIS.

'Tis but cypresses whispering " Here is a bridal ! " to cypresses round.

MAIDEN.

Thou hast rent from side to side my cloak !   Other robe have I none !

DAPHNIS.

A new one I'll give to my bride, an ampler-falling one.   60

MAIDEN.

Now lavish of everything—not a grain of salt by-and-by !

DAPHNIS.

Oh would that my soul I could bring, and add to my gifts heaped high !

MAIDEN.

Artemis, frown not, I pray, at thy votaress false to her vow !

DAPHNIS.

Unto Eros a calf will I slay, and to Aphrodite a cow.

MAIDEN.

A maiden I came ; I depart a woman now to my door !

DAPHNIS.

Nay, the queen of a husband's heart ; a mother, a maid no more.

  So each unto other the young and fair were whispering low :
Together enraptured they clung in secret spousals so.
She rose and departed at last, and to pasture her sheep she hied,   [70
With eyes for shame down-cast, thoughts glowing with wifehood's pride :
To the herds of his cattle he passed, heart-glad for his new-won bride.

IDYLL XXVIII.

A poem which accompanied the poet's present of an ivory distaff to Theugenis, the wife of his friend Nicias the physician.

O DISTAFF, gear to spinners dear, gift of Athena's hands
To all whose will is to fulfil true woman's holiest mission,
Fear not to fare with me to where old Neileus' city stands,
And rushes screen the Cyprian Queen, a shrined celestial vision.
From Heaven's King fair voyaging to yonder bourn I pray,
With joy to see joy meeting me in eyes of Nicias beaming—
That hallowed flower which decks the bower where rings the Graces' lay.
And thee, far-brought and travail-wrought from ivory white-gleaming,
To Nicias' bride I'll give, to glide between her fingers fair,
With her to spin the cloaks wherein men walk in goodly vesture,   10
And sheeny gleams, like rippling streams, of raiment women wear.
For, though men reap from mother-sheep the harvest of the pasture
Twice yearly, this shall Theugenis the dainty-ankled hold
Not store too much, so skilled her touch, so wifely-wise her spirit.
I would not bear thee, friend, to where dwell matrons idle-souled :
For thou and I be brethren, by the birth-land both inherit.
To found thine home did Archias roam from queenly Corinth's shore
In Sicily's heart to build a mart, home of a people glorious.
But, exiled now, abide shalt thou with one whose healing lore
Aye brings release from fell disease, o'er pains of men victorious.   20
Miletus sweet her guest shall greet ; Ionian shalt thou be.
No rock like this of Theugenis or dame or damsel knoweth !
Thou shalt be her remembrancer of friendship, song, and me.
Who looks soe'er on thee shall bear his witness—" Great grace goeth
With gifts, though ne'er so small—so fair the honour love bestoweth."

IDYLL XXIX.

Love's pleading.

IF truth be born of wine, as proverbs say,
Believe me now, for wine inspires the lay.
All my soul's secret will I tell to thee.
Thou wilt not give thine whole heart unto me,
I know : my life, to this thy beauty thrall,
Is but half life, the rest is ruin all.
When thou dost smile, my day is heaven-bright ;
When thou dost frown, 'tis overpalled with night.
How canst thou torture thus a loving heart ?
Nay, hear me—let me claim a mentor's part :   10
Thou wilt be happier—grateful, it may be :
Build one nest with me in one sheltering tree,
Whither shall climb no serpent jealousy.
Ah, now thou sittest on this bough to-day,
On that to-morrow, never at one stay !
A stranger sees and praises that sweet face,
And lo, is as a friend of olden days,
And thy first love—is lost mid waifs and strays !
I am too low—thine eyes look far above !
Nay, choose thine equal for a life-long love.   20
Then shall thy name as ointment be outpoured ;
Then shall Love be to thee no tyrant lord,
Love, who can set men's hearts beneath his heel,
Love, who has turned to wax this heart of steel.
Ah, by thy soft lips I beseech thee, dear,
Remember thou wert younger yester-year !
No spell may keep grey hairs and wrinkles back :
Youth's vanished steps may never hunter track,

Never, for on his shoulders pinions rise :
Too slow are we to catch the bird that flies. 30
Ah, think on this, smile one relenting smile,
And love me, as I love thee without guile.
So we, when all thy youth has fled away,
Shall love as lovers loved in olden day.
But if thou cast unto the winds my plea,
And say in wrath, " Fool, wherefore trouble me ? "—
Now for the Golden Apples would I go
For thee, bring Cerberus up from shades below ;
Then, though thou calledst to me from thy door,
I would not stir : mine heart should ache no more. 40

IDYLL XXX.

Love's misgivings. The same liberty has been taken in this version as in that of Idyll XXIII.

ALAS for me ! my heart is sick and sore,
Sick of love's fever thirty days and more !
  High as my heart her stature is, all grace
From head to heel ; smiles glorify her face :—
Ah me ! 'tis now a smile and now a frown !
Ere long not even sleep my cares will drown.
Yestreen she passed, from 'neath drooped lashes shot
One glance, ashamed to meet mine, flushing hot.
Then, oh, love more than ever gripped mine heart !
Home, with heart wounded, gnawed, did I depart.   10
Then sternly I arraigned my erring soul :
" Why do this ?—what shall be thy folly's goal ?
Art blind ?—thy temples now are silver-grey.
Think, think !—'tis time—face, form, are old to-day ;
And yet a young man's part thou needs must play !
Thou canst not see that better far it were
To turn thy back on Love's fear, hope, despair.
She—like a flying hart her days bound on :
To-morn afar will her light sails have flown.
Leave her her youth !—'tis brief as summer-flowers.   20
But thou—this brooding passion still devours
Thine inmost soul : dreams haunt thy nightly rest :
A whole year will not heal thy fevered breast."
  So—and with many more words—did I chide.
" Who thinks to vanquish Love," mine heart replied,—
" Love the Spell-weaver,—in conceit he tells
By ranks of nine the night's star-sentinels.
Whether I will or no, my neck must strain
Under Love's yoke : so doth the God ordain
By whom great Zeus, yea, Cypris, are o'erthrown.   30
Leaf of a day, by a mere wind-puff strown
On earth, where'er he willeth am I blown."

IDYLL XXXI.

The arraignment and acquittal of the boar that slew Adonis.

CYTHEREA beheld where mangled
   In death Adonis lay,
Saw the love-locks matted and tangled,
   The rose-cheeks ashen-grey ;
And she spake to her winged Loves, crying :
   " Go, bring me the murderer boar ! "
And they flew forth questing, and flying
      The wildwood o'er.

That caitiff boar, they found him,
   And shackles and fetters they threw   10
On him : one with a halter bound him
   And onward the captive drew.
One followed behind, assailing
   His flanks with the arrow-points keen ;
And the beast went cowering, quailing,
      For he feared Love's Queen.

Aphrodite the judge is speaking—
   " O vilest of brute-beasts born,
Was the scathe to his thigh of thy wreaking ?
   By thee was my lover torn ? "   20
And the boar made answer, replying :
   " Cytherea, I swear unto thee
By thyself, by the youth here lying,
      By these chains upon me,

And by these thine hunters moreover—
   Never I thought to smite
Adonis thy beautiful lover !
   As a statue he stood in my sight ;
And I loved with a flame all-consuming,
   I was frenzied with longing to kiss   30
His thigh in bare loveliness blooming ;
      And my tusk—did this !

Take these, Queen Cypris, and tear them
   For punishment forth, cut away—
What have I to do to wear them ?—
   These tusks love so could betray !
And if these will suffice not to render
   Requital, O deal like doom
To the lips that would kiss that splendour—
      How dared they presume ? "

Then Cypris in pity forgave him ;   40
   And she spake to the Loves : " Loose ye
The fetters wherein ye drave him
   Hither, and set him free."
In her train ever afterward pacing,
   To the forest he would not return,
But where Love's fire hottest was blazing,
      There still did he burn.

FRAGMENT FROM THE "BERENICE."

IF for wealth and for rich sea-spoil any seeketh with prayer and vow,
Any man who must live by the toil of the sea, and whose nets are his
    plough,
To this Goddess at dead of night for sacrifice let him bring
That sacred fish named "White," for 'tis brightest of all—then fling
His nets to the deep ; so the toiler shall reap rich harvesting.

INSCRIPTIONS.

I.

For the basrelief of a rural altar.

BRIGHT roses dew-besprent, sweet tufted thyme are we heaping
    On the altar, thereon to the Muses, the Queens of Helicon, spread ;
And for thee, O Pythian Healer, dark bay-boughs heavy-sweeping,
    For with garlands of this doth the Rock of Delphi crown thine head.
And yonder white horned goat, at the uttermost sprays upleaping
    Of the terebinth even now, shall stain thine altar red.

II.

For an offering dedicated to a temple.

Daphnis, the white-limbed herdman, from whose fair reed-pipes sweetly
    Ring pastoral strains, unto Pan doth all his treasures bring—
His piercèd reeds, keen dart, and the staff that smites hares featly,
    Fawnskin, and scrip wherein apples were borne, love's offering.

III.

For a picture.

Ha, Daphnis, asleep !   While thy nets on the hillside staked are forsaken,
  All weary-limbed thou art resting here on the leaf-strewn ground.
But the hunt is up !   It is thou art the quarry of Pan !—O waken !—
  And Priapus, whose winsome brows with the gold-blossomed ivy are
    crowned.
They are bursting together into thy cave !—flee, ere thou be taken !
  Shake off the heavy fetters of slumber wherein thou art bound !

IV.

For a way-side shrine.

When thou hast reached, by the oak-trees, goat-herd, the long lane's
    turning,
  An image there shalt thou find new-carven of fig-tree wood ;
Three-legged is it, rough with the bark, and earless, but plain for dis-
    cerning
  'Tis the mystic virtue creative, the symbol of fatherhood.
A hallowed precinct encompasseth this, and a stream ever-flowing
  Falls from the rocks, and around it a bower of greenness springs,
A bower of the bay, of the myrtle, of cypress odour-blowing ;
  And around it the rippling vine, the mother of clusters, flings
Her tendrils ; and there are the merles with clarion voices hailing   [10
  The spring, with the fluctuant music of changing and wavering notes ;
And the soft brown nightingales there are with sorrow's antiphons wailing,
  Pouring unceasingly forth the sweet sad strain from their throats.
There sit thou down, and to comely Priapus perform this mission—
  Pray him to rid mine heart of its hunger of love for my fair :
I will offer a kid to him then.   But and if he deny my petition,
  And if yet I shall win my love, triple gifts will I bring to him there ;
For a heifer, a goat, and a stall-fed lamb, for love's fruition,
  Will I sacrifice then—and oh, may he graciously hear this prayer !

V.

For a picture or basrelief.

Come, for the Nymphs' sake, play on thy reed-pipes consonant-singing
    Some strain of delight ; and I, my prentice fingers shall sweep
The harp-strings ; and Daphnis the herd, as his lips are with melody
    winging
    The breath of the wax-knit pipes, true measure with us shall keep.
We will stand 'neath the dense-leaved oak, and our notes through his
    cavern ringing
    Shall cheat the goat-footed Forest-lord of his noontide sleep.

VI.

For the tomb of a little girl.

Alas for thee, Thyrsis ! Wherein shall it profit thee, though with thy
    mourning
    The sight of both thine eyes be in tears consumed away ?
Thy kidling, the fair and young, is gone !—whence is no returning
    She is gone !—for the jaws of the ruthless wolf have snapped on the
    prey.
Dolefully howl thy dogs—what avails it ? The pyre of her burning
    Hath left of thy vanished love nor bone nor ashes grey.

VII.

For the pedestal of a statue of Aesculapius.

Far as Miletus the Son of Pæĕon, the Master of Healing,
    Hath come : to be guest of a healer of sickness the God is content ;
For Nicias daily draws nigh him, with sacrifices appealing,
    And hath caused to be carved this statue of cedar sweet of scent.
Richly he promised to guerdon Eëtion's hand, for revealing
    What a sculptor can do, and his uttermost art on the work hath he
    spent.

VIII.

For a traveller's tomb.

Orthon of Syracuse, stranger, warns from the Land of Shadows—
 " Go not abroad on a night of storm when merry with wine ;
For thus did I come by mine end.   For my fatherland's wide-stretching
    meadows,
 A corner of alien soil—such scanty vesture is mine."

IX.

For a merchant's tomb.

Man, have regard to thy life : on the sea launch forth not, unheeding
 Of season due : for the life of man is at best but short.
Cleonicus the hapless, thou unto Thasos the sunny speeding
 Didst sail with thy merchandise forth from a Coele-Syrian port :
With thy merchandise thou, Cleonicus, didst follow the Pleiads' leading ;
 For they sank in the sea—and thou didst sink in the selfsame sort !

X.

For a basrelief of the Muses.

O Goddesses Nine, unto you this marble group, the oblation
 Of love and of gratitude, doth the minstrel Xenocles raise—
Yea, a minstrel, and none will gainsay !   To the Queens of his inspiration
 He forgets not to render their due, who gave him his crown of praise.

XI.

For a physiognomist's tomb.

This is Eusthenes' tomb : men's natures his wisdom could read in their
    faces,
 He looked in their eyes, and his shrewdness straightway discerned the
    mind.
Here friends have buried him, far from his home's familiar places.
 A poet he was, and to brother poets exceeding kind.
The wise man even in death thus love's remembrance graces.
 Frail was his form, but many a loving friend did he find.

XII.

For a statue with a tripod.

This tripod and statue, O Wine-god dearest of Gods all-glorious,
    The chorus-master Demomeles dedicates as thy due.
No prize won his chorus of boys : with the chorus of men victorious
    He stood, for that which was beauteous and best-befitting he knew.

XIII.

For a statue of Aphrodite.

This is Cypris—not She of the Street—'tis the Goddess Celestial ; revere
    her.
Pure-hearted Chrysogone set this statue up in the hall
Of Amphicles.   Hers are his children and life, none nearer nor dearer.
    Ever to these, as the years fleet on, better days befall ;
For, Queen, they begin each year with thy worship.   The true god-fearer
    Hath the blessing of all the Immortals, and prosperous fortune withal.

XIV.

For a tomb.

An infant son didst thou leave, and thyself in thy youth didst perish,
    Eurymedon : this tomb only on earth did thy dead frame find.
But thou, thou art throned mid the Sons of the Gods, and thy people shall
    cherish
    Thy child for thy sake, ever bearing his noble father in mind.

XV.

For a gallant soldier's tomb.

Now shall I know if thou reverencest the brave when he dieth,
    Or whether from thee like honour, wayfarer, the coward hath won.
" Hail to this tomb ! " wilt thou cry, if thine heart be true, for it lieth
    Light on the sacred head of a hero, Eurymedon.

XVI.

For a child's tomb.

Our girlie hath left us untimely ; our floweret whose years were seven !
  Many a year ere her time into Hades' gulf did she sink—
Alas for my sweet!—for she pined for the baby-brother given
  Not two years ere of the cup he drank from which all lips shrink.
Oh my poor darling !   Oh my lost Doveling !—how close doth Heaven
  Set by the children of men the draught they abhor to drink !

XVII.

For a statue of Anacreon.

Gaze on this statue, stranger, earnestly ;
    And, when thou hast returned home, shalt thou say :
" Anacreon's statue in Teos did I see,
  A poet passing all of olden day."
Add this—" A friend to all young hearts was he ; "
  And the whole man thou truly wilt portray.

XVIII.

For a statue in a theatre.

In Dorian speech we sing the Dorian, Epicharmus, he
    Who first invented Comedy.
O Bacchus, here in bronze his counterfeit presentment stands
    Reared in thy courts by loving hands
Of exiles who in Syracuse have sojourned ; Coan men
    Rear it to their own citizen.
Rich wealth had he of poesy, wherewith he wont to crown
    The love that cherished his renown :
With many a golden sentence did he made our lives sublime.
    Thanks unto him, thanks through all time !   10

XIX.

For the tomb of an old servant.

The child Medeius rears this tomb beside the public way :
    " CLEITA," his nurse's name, is graven there,
    A Thracian : we requite her loving care
Thus of our boy. " Ah, good and faithful servant ! " still we say.

XX.

For the statue of an original poet.

Stand and behold the poet of old, Archilochus, he
    Who sang in Iambics, whose myriad renown
    From the sunrise hath passed to the sun's going-down.
Of the Muses beloved, of Apollo approved was he verily,
    So practised, so cunning of touch he became
    In fashioning song, and in chanting the same.

XXI.

For the statue of an epic poet.

Lo, this is he who sang of Zeus's scion
The swift of hand, the queller of the lion.
He first of bards in that far-distant day,
Peisander of Cameirus, sang this lay,
Sang all the toils wrought by the Hero's hand.
Therefore, know thou, the people of this land
Here set him up in bronze, when months had fled
Many, and many years passed o'er the dead.

XXII.

For the tomb of a satiric poet, who had been the terror of " respectable rogues.

The bard Hipponax 'neath this stone doth lie.
If thou be knave, to this tomb draw not nigh :
If thou be true man, sprung from honest sires,
Sit fearless down, yea, sleep, if so thy soul desires.

XXIII.

For the booth of a money-changer and banker.

This bank dealeth fairly alike with the citizen and with the stranger :
Whatsoe'er thou hast paid is repaid when accounts are balanced aright.
Other bankers may shuffle and cheat ; with Caïcus there is no danger :
Thou canst trust him to render thine own to thee—yea, in the darkness
of night !

XXIV.

For a volume of his own poems.

I am Theocritus, I, who indited these songs : far other
Was the mighty Chian ; but I am of Syracuse, one of the throng.
My father Praxagoras was, and renownèd Philinna my mother.
Never I claimed for mine own one line of another's song.

THE IDYLLS OF BION.

IDYLL I.

The Dirge for Adonis, the lover of Aphrodite.

WOE for Adonis dead !   Adonis the Fair is gone !
Adonis the Fair is sped !   The Loves re-echo my moan.
No longer in purple pall, Aphrodite, sleep on thy bed !
Wake, shroud thee in vesture of night !   O wake unto misery, smite
On thy breast !   Cry aloud unto all : " Adonis the Fair is dead ! "
  " *Woe for Adonis !* " *I sigh.* " *Woe !* " *wailing Eroses cry.*
Lies Adonis the Fair on the height of the hills ; in his thigh is death—
His white thigh gashed by the white tusk !   Cypris anguisheth
As his soul flutters forth on the air : the blood dark-crimson is flowing
Over the skin snow-fair, and heavy his eyelids are growing.   10
The rose from his lip is flying ; there even the living glow
Of the kiss of the Deathless is dying, which Love's Queen cannot forego.
Still sweet unto Cypris is this, though lost from his lips is the breath.
But Adonis knew not—her kiss lay cold on the gate of death !
  " *Woe for Adonis !* " *I sigh.* " *Woe !* " *wailing Eroses cry.*
A cruel wound and a fierce hath the thigh of Adonis the Fair ;
But a deeper wound, that doth pierce to the heart, Cytherea must bear.
Drearly his sleuth-hounds bayed round their loved lord lying there.
Weeps, wails each Mountain-maid for the dead.   With unbraided hair
Aphrodite is wandering round wild thickets, frenzy-borne,   20
Grief-stricken, with tresses unbound, unsandalled ; and many a thorn
Stabbeth her, blossometh red with the sacred blood of the Queen.
On through the long glades sped, with wailing wild and keen,

On her morning-land lover she crieth, and calleth the boy in vain,
The while the dark blood dyeth his waist, and the crimson stain
From his thighs stealeth up to his chest and the snow-white spaces below
Death-stricken Adonis' breast, flushed now with the purple flow.
  " Woe is thee, Cytherea ! " I sigh. " Woe ! " wailing Eroses cry.
Gone is her love from her arms, gone with him her beauty divine.
O Cypris, what heavenly charms, while lived Adonis, were thine !   30
Cytherea's beauty hath died with Adonis—alas the day !
Wail oak-tree and mountain-side : " Alas for Adonis ! " they say.
Sobbing are rill and river for Aphrodite's pain :
Mid lone hills fountains shiver down tears for Adonis slain.
All flowers for anguish are flushing red : Cythera thrills[1]
With the storm of a wild dirge rushing through all her glens and hills :
  " Cytherea is woe—he is dead !   Fair Adonis is Hades-ward sped ! "
And in answer did Echo cry : " He hath perished, Adonis the fair ! "
Who had wept not of sympathy for Cypris' love, her despair ?
When she saw her Adonis' wound, when she knew it unstanchably
        deep,   40
When she saw the life-blood around that thigh all-nerveless creep,
" Adonis," she cried, " O stay ! "—and her arms abroad she cast—
" Stay, hapless Adonis !—delay till we meet for the last time, the last !
That thee in mine arms I may take, that my lips to thy lips I may
        press !
For a moment, Adonis, O wake for this one last caress !
Kiss me so long, and no more, as the life of a kiss doth abide,
Till thy breath from thy soul shall pour between my lips, and shall slide
Down to mine heart, and my soul in the rapture thereof will I steep,
And so shall I drain love's bowl, and this treasure-kiss will I keep,
As Adonis himself, for aye—since thou, lost love, dost flee,   50
O Adonis, dost flee far away unto Acheron, far from me
To the cruel King all hate, and in wretchedness I live on,
A Goddess, forbidden by Fate to follow where thou art gone.
Take my lover, Persephone, spare not !—thou far surpassest me
In might.   All things most fair drift down at the last unto thee.

  1. The island sacred to Aphrodite, from which she was named Cytherea.

All-wretched am I : my yearning hunger of heart cannot rest :
For Adonis the unreturning I wail with despairing breast.
O thrice-desired, thou hast died !   As a dream hath vanished all
My desire !   I am widowed ; with void hands loiter the Loves in mine hall.
My Girdle of Beauty is gone with thee !   Oh hunter rash !   60
So lovely, what set thee on in battle with brutes to clash ? "
So mourned Cytherea, and so the Eroses answering wailed :
  " *Cypris is woe—he is dead !   Fair Adonis is Hades-ward sped !* "
A tear from the Paphian shall flow for each blood-drop that failed
From the veins of Adonis.   They turn to flowers, on the earth as they
      light.
Red roses for blood-drops burn, each tear is a windflower white.
  I wail for Adonis' sake !   The life of the lovely hath flown !
No more in the forest-brake, O Cypris, thy lover bemoan.
Unmeet is a wild leaf-bed for Adonis thy love to be strown !
For Adonis the slain be spread thy couch, Cytherea, thine own.   70
Fair dead !—O, in death still fair, he lieth as one asleep !
Where he slumbered once, lay him there, and the silken coverlets heap
Whereon in thine arms he hath lain through the darkness glory-starred,
On the golden bed still fain of Adonis, though now death-marred.
Garlands and blossoms O cast on him !   All sweet things in that hour
Died, when the beautiful passed, and faded every flower.
Drop myrrh-scent down on thy sweet, all orient unguents rain—
No ! let perfumes to nothingness fleet, for Adonis, thy myrrh, is slain !
  In purple arrayed, as in sleep flower-soft Adonis lies,
And around him the Eroses weep with exceeding bitter cries.   80
They have shorn for Adonis their hair : on his shafts one trampleth, in
      token
Of grief, on his bow one ; there his quiver another hath broken.
The sandal doth one unlace of Adonis, another brings
In a golden vase spring-water, one cleanseth the stains of slaughter ;
One fanneth Adonis' face, as he had but swooned, with his wings.
  " *Woe is thee ! Cytherea !* " I sigh.   " *Woe !* " *wailing Eroses cry.*
All Hymen's torches are lying quenched now beside the door :
His wreath-flowers scattered are dying.   The bridal-chant no more,

" Hymen, O Hymen ! " is ringing from glad lips, well-a-day !
A new song, alas ! are they singing for Adonis—no Hymen-lay !   90
 Tis the Graces' song of despair, and for Cinyras' son are they sighing :
" Dead is Adonis the Fair ! " ever each unto other is crying.
O wild and high is it scaling the sky—not Paeon's praise !—
For Adonis the Muses are wailing, for Adonis the dirge they upraise.
They sing of the lovely, the dear ; but nothing he heareth of this—
Not that he wills not to hear, but in Cora's prison he is.
   Cease now, Cytherea, from mourning ; for to-day from thy wailing
      refrain.
When the dark day cometh, returning a year hence, then weep again.

IDYLL II.

*A fragment of the story of Achilles, whom his mother Thetis concealed, dis-
guised as a girl, among the daughters of the king of Scyros, that he might
not be taken to Troy, where, by the decree of fate, death awaited him.*

MYRSON.

WILT thou, O Lycidas, sing me a sweet Sicilian lay,
Such melting, heart-ravishing thing as the Cyclops once on a day
Sang, to allure with his strain Galatea beside the sea ?

LYCIDAS.

Yea, Myrson, myself were fain to pipe.   What song shall it be ?

MYRSON.

   The song of Scyros be this, the lay of love's delight,
Of Achilles' stolen kiss, and the stolen joys of the night,
Of the prince disguised as a maid, and in damsels' vesture arrayed,
And how Deïdameia, amid Lycomedes' daughters alone
Charmed forth the secret hid in the heart of Peleus' son.

LYCIDAS.

With Helen the neat-herd had fled, and his prey unto Ida afar, 10
For a grief to Oenone, had led : rose Sparta in wrath unto war,
And she summoned all the array of Achaia ; of Hellas not one,
Nor Mycenae, said her nay : of Elis, of Sparta, was none
That abode in his halls, that hung back shrinking from war's red field.
Achilles alone was among Lycomedes' daughters concealed ;
And, instead of weapons, the wool did he handle, his fingers white
Of a maiden's labours were full ; yea, a maiden he was to the sight,
And a woman's soft ways he assumed, like the rest : his comely face
With roses and lilies bloomed, and his feet were schooled to pace
In maiden wise ; o'er his hair the veil of a woman he drew. 20
Yet the heart of a man he bare, and the love of a man he knew.
And from dawning till eventide by Deïdameia's side
Would he sit, oft kissing her hand, and oftentimes would he raise
Her loom's fair web, and scanned, and its beautiful threads would he
 praise.
In her only companionship had he joy, and was seeking aye
With her to attain twinned sleep : then he spake unto her on a day :
" Lo, other thy sisters twain by twain ever take their rest ;
But alone I only remain, and alone thou slumberest.
We be maidens, thou and I, like-aged, both fair to behold ;
Yet sleeping alone dost thou lie ! 'Tis the work of the crafty-souled, 30
Thy nurse, her malignancy, that forbids me still to enfold
Thee in mine arms, and nigh to mine heart my belovèd to hold " . . .

 (Cetera desunt.)

IDYLL III.

The rival charms of the Seasons.

CLEODAMAS.

SPRING—winter—Myrson my friend—or autumn, or summer's fire—
Which of these dost thou most commend, whose coming dost most desire ?

Is it summer, when perfected are all our labours at last ?
Is it autumn, when hunger hath fled from men as a dream that is past ?
Is it winter of toilless days, when a man, as though spell-bound,
Sitteth, charmed by the ingle's blaze to oblivion of labour's round ?
Or is fair Spring Lady of Pleasure to thee ?   Thine heart's choice tell,
Forasmuch as for converse our leisure in this hour serveth well.

MYRSON.

  For men is it nowise meet on the works of the Gods to pass
Judgment ; for holy and sweet be they all : yet, Cleodamas,   10
For thy sake I consent to say of these which pleaseth me best.
I would not have summer alway, by the sun's heat scorched and op-
    pressed ;
Nor autumn's bountihead, for her fruits oft gender disease ;
And ruinous winter I dread—not in snow and in ice would I freeze !
Spring, thrice-desired, thrice-sweet, be with me all through the year !
Then frost is there none, nor the heat of the sun is a burden to bear.
Teeming in spring is the soil, all sweet things blossom then,
And the hours of sleep and of toil are evenly meted to men.

IDYLL IV.

The young fowler and the winged Eros.

A FOWLER—a mere lad yet—as chasing the birds he hied
Through a woodland glade with his net, amidst of a box-tree spied
Love the light-pinioned : he sate on a bough, and the boy's eyes
    gleamed
With joy at the sight, so great and so goodly a bird it seemed.
Each unto other he fitted the joints of his fowling-reed,
And on Love, as hither he flitted and thither, kept watch with heed.

But the lad grew angered at last, seeing end of his labour was none.
He caught up his reeds, and fast to a ploughman grey did he run,
Who had taught him the craft of the snare, and he told of his hopes be-
    guiled,
And he pointed to Love sitting there in the tree. But the old man
    smiled,   20
As he shook his silver hair, and answer he made to the child :
"Chase him not !   From this hunting forbear ; for this is no bird of the
    wild.
'Tis a baneful creature : O flee him !   Thou shalt be fortunate
While he goeth untaken of thee.   If thou come to man's estate,
This same who hath flitted and fled thee, himself unbidden shall come
On a sudden to thee : on thine head shall he settle then—for thy doom.

IDYLL V.

The herdman-minstrel and his pupil.

GREAT Cypris stood by mine head as I lay in slumber-land,
And the young babe Eros she led with her lovely-moulded hand :
Earthward-bowed was his face ; and on this wise spake she to me :
" Dear herdman, teach Love, for a grace unto me, to sing like thee."
She spake, and was gone ; and I, like a child in simplicity, sought
To teach him my minstrelsy, as though Love fain would be taught.
How Pan of the cross-flute was sire, how the flute for Athene outpealed,
How Hermes devised the lyre, how Apollo the harp revealed—
All this to teach him I strove ; but he heeded my lessoning naught,
But still sang lays of love unto me : the desires he taught   10
Of men, of Immortals above, and the deeds by his mother wrought.
And forgot was my learning's store that to Eros I fain would impart—
But the music of Love's heart-lore, all this sank into my heart.

IDYLL VI.

Eros and the Muses are allies.

THE Muses from Love's wild wings shrink never away in affright,
But they love him with love that springs from the heart, and they follow
    his flight.
But who beareth a loveless heart, and yet would mimic their strain,
From him do they hold them apart, and from teaching him aught they
    refrain.
He whose spirit is swept by the wind of love, till its strings sing sweet,
Him meet they with eager mind, as when hurrying rivers meet.
I am witness thereof, and the thing hereby is certified :
If of any mortal I sing, or of any Immortal beside,
Then falters my tongue, and no more can I sing as theretofore ;
But and if of Eros again I sing, and of Lycidas,   10
Outfloweth a jubilant strain, through my lips exulting to pass.

IDYLL VII.

*How vain are men's hopes and aims. Compare LXXVI, LXXVII, of
"In Memoriam."*

I KNOW not—'tis but vanity
    To strive to see beyond our ken—
    If these my songs shall win from men
Renown in ages yet to be.

To me they seem fair—O, I thought
    They breathed the Muse's breath divine :
    But if they touch no heart but mine,
My work is vain, my life is naught.

Ah, if but Cronos' Son, or Fate,
    The mutable, to men had lent
    Two lives, that mirth and merriment
Might fill one half this mortal state,

While half in grinding toil were passed,
    Then might one labour on, content,
    With eyes on that far future bent
When he should reap good things at last.

But, seeing the high Gods ordain
    That man shall live but once his life—
    A short span that, and misery-rife—
Why should we toil, sad hearts, in vain ?

To what end should we sell our souls
    For lucre, for the petty schemes
    Of life, and waste ourselves in dreams
Of winning wealth—that goal of goals ?

Ah, we forget, all, all forget
    That we are doomed, or soon or late,
    To die, and from that sentence Fate
Grants but a brief, brief respite yet.

FRAGMENTS.

I.

HAPPY are they that love, when heart may in heart confide.
Happy was Theseus, so long as Peirithous stood by his side,
Though together adown to the mansion of Hades the ruthless they hied.
Orestes was happy amidst hard men who were haters of strangers,
Since Pylades chose to share his journeyings and his dangers.
Blest was Achilles Aeacus' son, while lived his friend—
Yea, happy in death ; he avenged that friend's dire doom ere the end.

II.

Hesperus, golden light of the Foam-born Goddess thou,
Dear sacred jewel that Night dark-vestured hath set on her brow !
More faint than the moon dost thou glow, yet all stars dost transcend.
Hail, kind one ! As singing I go to my love's cottage-door, O lend
Thy light unto me in the place of the moon ; for it was but to-day
That again she began her race, and hath set too soon. My way
Is no thief's path ; no night-wayfarer hath hurt of me ;
But a lover am I, and 'tis right that lovers find grace of thee.

III.

O gentle Cyprian Queen, Zeus' Child, from the sea who didst rise,
Why is thy wrath so keen against men and the Lords of the Skies ?
Too mild was the word—why *hate* us so fiercely that thou shouldest give
Birth to a curse so great as is Love unto all that live,
That cruel, tyrannous one ?—so lovely, so loveless of heart !
Thou hast given him wings—ah why ?—and the arrows afar that fly,
So that none of us all may shun this child's most bitter dart.

IV.

(*From " The Death of Hyacinthus," whom by misadventure Apollo slew
with a cast of his quoit*).

  All speechless Phoebus stood in that great anguish of heart :
All healing herbs he sought, tried all the leech's art ;
With ambrosia and nectar for salves he anointed all the wound ;
But against the stroke of fate unavailing are all salves found.

V.

I will yonder take my way to the seaward-dipping slope,
  And there will I murmur my lay by the beach and the sighing sand,
And to Galatea will pray, to the ruthless—ah, sweet Hope,
  I will follow thy starry ray till on eld's last verge I stand !

VI.

It beseems not to seek to a craftsman, my friend, for each small need,
Nor for every matter to lean on another. Thy pipe of reed
Fashion thyself : 'twere an easy task, in veriest deed.

VII.

Let Eros summon the Muses, the Muses bring Love in their train !
May the Muses bestow on me song, the gift that I yearn to gain !
Sweet song !—there is no more pleasant salve than this for pain.

VIII.

Drops ceaselessly falling, as sayeth the saw, ever one after one,
Will carve out a hollow at last in the face of the flinty stone.

IX.

Ah, leave me not unguerdoned ! Song won its fitting meed
Even for Phoebus ; and honour betters the noblest deed.

X.

The glory of woman is beauty bright ;
The glory of man is his bodily might.

XI.

In all labour, if God so will, there is profit. All ways we wend
Are smoothed by the Blessèd Ones, and brought to a prosperous end.

THE IDYLLS OF MOSCHUS.

IDYLL I.

Aphrodite proclaims a search for Eros the Runaway.

FAR and wide did the Cyprian raise for Eros the hue and cry—
" Hath any, where meet three ways, seen Eros wandering by ?
Truant from me he is.　His reward shall who finds not lack :
The guerdon is Cypris' kiss.　But and if thou shalt bring him back,
Thou shalt earn not a kiss alone, O stranger, but more, far more !
This child shall be easily known ; thou wouldst mark him amidst a score :
Not white is his skin, but it seems like flame ; keen glances are darted
From his eyes, and therein fire gleams : he is sweet-tongued, evil-hearted ;
For his thought and his word are not one ; as honey his speech is sweet,
But his wrath is a flame that none can tame : he is ever a cheat ;　　10
He is truthless, a babe whose breast is all guile, and cruel his sport :
His head is lovely-tressed, but he eyes thee in impudent sort.
Tiny his small hands are, but they speed shafts far from the string,
Yea, even to Acheron, far as the heart of Hades' King.
Of raiment his body is bare, but his spirit is veilèd close :
He is winged like a bird of the air, and he swoops now on these, now on
　　those,
Upon men, upon women, and there doth he nestle, till each heart glows.
He beareth a tiny bow, and a shaft on the string ever lies :
Right small is the arrow, but oh, in its flight doth it leap to the skies.
On his back is a quiver of gold, and bitter the arrow-reeds be　　20
Therein, with the which this bold boy oftentimes wounds even me.
Cruel they all are, all his weapons ; but all are outdone
By his torch ; it is passing small, yet it kindleth the very sun.

If thou catch him, in pity spare not, but bind and bring hither the child.
If weeping thou see him, beware lest thou be by his tears beguiled.
If he laugh, still hitherward hale him ; and if he would kiss thee, beware
That kiss, for therein is thy bale, for a drug of enchantment is there.
If he say, ' Take torch, bow, quiver : all freely I give for thine hire,'
Those treacherous gifts touch never ; they all are dipped in fire."

IDYLL II.

Europa and the Bull.

To Europa did Cypris send a sweet dream long ago,
When the night drew on to its end, when near was the dawning-glow,
When sleep that relaxeth the strained limbs sweeter than honey lies
On the eyelids, and softly chained by its fetters are weary eyes,
When, like sheep from the meadows, true dreams out of shadows of
    darkness rise.
Even then, as lay on her bed 'neath her home's roof slumbering
Europa, a maid unwed, the daughter of Phoinix the King,
Two mainlands appeared before her ; contending for her they were,
One Asia, the oversea shore the other : the forms they bare
Of women—an alien she, and she of her own land sprung,   10
As it seemed, and passionately to the maiden her child she clung ;
And ever she cried : " I bore her, I also gave her the breast ! "
But the other with strong hands tore her away, and strove to wrest
The maid, nothing loth, from her ward ; and still, with insistent cries
Said : " Zeus the Aegis-lord hath decreed Europa my prize ! "
   And the maiden awoke, and quaking sprang from her bed ; with fear
Her heart beat hard, for a waking vision did all appear.
Long silent sat she there, amazed and wide-eyed : still
On the women twain did she stare, for her vision they seemed to fill.
And at last did the maiden cry in her fear and her wonderment :   20
" Ah, who of the Dwellers on High these phantoms to me hath sent ?

What manner of dreams with dismay have thrilled me, here mid my
    bowers
On my soft-strown bed as I lay and slept through the darkling hours ?
Now who was the alien dame whom I saw in the slumber-tide ?
How leapt in mine heart a flame of love !—how gracious-eyed
She gathered me unto her breast as with yearning of motherhood !
Ah, may the Gods ever-blest accomplish my dream in good ! "
  So spake she, and leapt to her feet, and she sought her companions dear,
High-born, to her heart most sweet, like-aged with herself to a year,
With whom she sported ever, when she stood for the dance ready-
    dight,   30
Or, where met the sea and the river, she bathed her body bright,
Or in odour-breathing meadows was wreathing the lilies white.
Full soon they appeared : in her hand did each fair maiden bear
A dainty flower-maund ; and forth to the meads did they fare
Which lay by the sea, where oft assembled that blithe band,
And joyed in the roses and soft-sighing plash of the surf on the sand.
With a basket all of gold in her hand Europa came ;
A marvel it was to behold ; 'twas the work of the Lord of Flame.
Unto Libya he gave it, the bride whom the Shaker of Earth had won :
And she unto lovely-eyed Telephassa gave it anon,   40
For by ties of blood were they bound : Telephassa her mother laid
That bright gift world-renowned in the hands of Europa the maid.
Work cunning and marvellous on its carven splendour shone.
Io, daughter of Inachus, was fashioned in gold thereon :
In the shape of a heifer still, of her woman's form bereft,
She roamed at her feet's wild will, and the salt sea-waves she cleft ;
Yea, as one swimming she seemed : the sea was fashioned in blue,
And overhanging it gleamed a cliff ; on its brow stood two
Men clasping hands, as they gazed on that seafaring marvel of kine.
There wrought was Zeus, and he raised full gently his hand divine   50
Unto Io the Heifer's brow upon Egypt's seven-channelled plain—
And lo, from a horned thing now is she changed to a woman again !
In silver the Nile-flood rolled, the heifer was wrought in brass,
But all of the purest gold the image of great Zeus was.

Round the curve of the maund, fair-crowned with the wreath of its shining
    rim,
The story of Hermes was found, and stretched out, slain by him,
Was Argus, with eyes beset that never were closed in sleep ;
And from where his blood gleamed wet on the crimsoned earth did there
    leap
A bird exulting in pride of pinions like flowers of the lea,
Spreading his tail forth wide, as a ship doth her sails on the sea :   60
Round the lip of the basket of gold did his compassing feathers meet.
A maund of such marvellous mould had Europa the fair and sweet.

    So when to the meads they were come with the starry blossoms bright,
In flowers of diverse bloom each maiden took her delight,
The narcissus odour-breathing, the hyacinth's purple bell,
The violet, the thyme close-wreathing the earth's face : gleamed that dell
With petals of children untold of the green spring-quickened mead.
And the incensed tresses of gold of the crocus were others with speed
Plucking in rivalry keen ; but amidst them the fair young queen,
As her fingers gathered the rose in its fiery splendour, shone   70
As amidst of the Graces shows unrivalled the Foam-born One.

    Ah, not long gladsome-souled amid flowers was she destined to tread,
Nor long unsullied to hold her girdle of maidenhead !
For the heart of Cronos' Son, so soon as he marked her, was swept
By the wind of Love, and was won his thrall by the shafts that leapt
From the Cyprian, who can subdue even Zeus, and only she.
Now therefore, lest he should rue fierce Hera's jealousy,
Of purpose withal to beguile the gentle heart of the maid,
He veiled his godhead awhile in the shape of a bull arrayed—   [80
No bull such as feedeth in stall, by whose strength is the earth's face rent
While the clods in sunder fall, as he haleth the plough fair-bent ;
No bull such as grazeth the pasture, no bull whose strong limbs strain,
Subdued to the will of a master, in dragging the laden wain.
Now all the rest of his frame was bright bay, save alone
Where a silver star's white flame in the midst of his forehead shone.
From his eyes that with soft fire gleamed the lightning of love out-
    streamed ;

And twin horns rose from his head branched evenly right and left,
Like the moon's crescent-tips dispread when her circle in twain is cleft.
   To the meadow he came by the beach ; and the maidens knew no fear
Of his coming, but woke in each a desire to draw more near,   90
And to touch that bull sweet-seeming. His breathing's fragrance went
Over the mead far-streaming, surpassing the flowers' rich scent.
He stood before the feet of Europa the noble and young,
And he licked her neck, and a sweet spell over her spirit he flung ;
And with lingering touch she caressed him, and wiped the plenteous flow
Of foam from his mouth, and pressed her lips to the star on his brow.
Gently the seeming-brute 'gan low : thou wouldst say 'twas the sound
Of a clear Mygdonian flute that murmured music round.
Down at her feet did he stoop, and he gazed appealingly,
Turning his neck, as to mean : " On my broad back throne thee, my
    queen ! "   100
And unto the heavy-tressed troop of her maiden friends did she cry :
" Hither, companions dear and young ! Now mount we arow
For disport on the bull bowed here : for us all is there room enow,
So huge a back boweth he ; like a ship on the strand it lies !
Tame is he and gentle to see, not like in any wise
Unto other bulls, but the heart of a man beats in him, of one
Who knoweth the righteous part, and he lacketh speech alone."
   So spake she, and smilingly herself on his back did she seat ;
And the rest, her fellows, drew nigh : but the bull straight leapt to his
    feet,
Having won his coveted prey, and swiftly drew nigh to the sea.   110
She turned her about in dismay, and to those dear friends cried she,
Outstretching her suppliant hands, but they strove to reach her in vain.
Spurned by his feet were the sands, like a dolphin he leapt o'er the main :
From wave to wave did he race with hooves unwetted of spray,
And ever the sea's broad face grew calm as he sped on his way.
All round did the sea-beasts leap before the feet divine ;
Glad dolphins rose from the deep and tumbled o'er surges of brine.
Rose Nereids up from their caves, and on huge sea-monsters seated
Over the flashing waves in triumph-procession fleeted.

And the Lord of the loud sea-thunder, the Earth-shaker, stood on the
    sea,   120
And he levelled the billows, and under his brother's feet made he
A straight sea-highway, and round him gathered a Triton-train,
Haunters of holy ground far under the deep-flowing main,
And from tapering conchs did they sound long notes of a bridal strain.
   But she, by the shape on-borne for a God's disguising wrought,
With the one hand grasped the horn of the bull, with the other upcaught
Her purple mantle's fold, that it might not trail out free
And be drenched by the waves untold and the silver spray of the sea.
By a following wind swelled wide her fluttering mantle blew
Sail-wise, and over the tide as wafted on wings she flew.   130
   But when far from her fatherland-shore she beheld her amidst of the
    deep,
Nor surf-lashed beach any more was seen, neither mountain-steep,
But only the sky overhead, and around sea measureless-wide,
She gazed about her in dread, and she lifted her voice and cried :
" O bull-god, whither dost bear me ?   Who art thou ?   On this strange
    path
With what wild feet dost thou fare, nor fearest the great sea's wrath ?
For the sea is the broad race-track for ships that the wind wafts on ;
But bulls in dread shrink back from the highway where foothold is
    none.
What drink is sweet unto thee ?—whereon in the sea canst thou feed ?
Ah, art thou a God ?—can it be ?—Gods only could do such deed !   140
Sea-dolphins can nowise pace the land, nor bulls can tread
The paths of the sea, but thou—over land-track and sea-track now
All dreadless dost thou race, by thine hooves as by oars on-sped.
Nay, haply yet wilt thou rise high over the grey sea-haze,
And wilt soar like a bird that flies fast onward by printless ways.
Oh evil-starred !—ah, woe is me, who have left the home
Of my sire far over the tide, have taken this bull for guide,
And on strange sea-faring go, and a friendless wanderer roam !
O Earth-shaker, thee I entreat, who art king of a grey salt realm,
Graciously now do thou meet me !—methinks I behold thee helm   150

This desperate voyage of mine, and thou makest my pathway plain !
Yea, not but with help divine do I traverse the rolling main."
  So spake she ; the broad-horned steer with a man's voice answered and
    said :
" O maiden, be thou of good cheer. Of the sea-surge have no dread.
I am Zeus' self, though, unto eyes that scan me how closely soe'er,
I seem but a bull. What guise I will have I power to wear.
Thy beauty hath spurred me on to measure these leagues of sea
In the shape of a bull. Anon shall the isle Crete welcome thee—
My foster-mother was she—and there shall thy bride-bower be,
And to strong sons world-renowned of me shalt thou yet give birth, 160
Unto great kings sceptre-crowned, who shall rule o'er the children of
    earth."
  So spake he, and all was fulfilled which he spake. Appeared the land
Of Crete : in such shape as he willed did Zeus before her stand.
Her zone he unbound, and spread by the Hours was their bridal-bed ;
And the erstwhile maiden there became great Zeus's bride,
And sons to Cronion she bare, and hers was a mother's pride.

IDYLL III.

The Lament for the poet Bion, whom envious rivals were said to have poisoned.

WAIL, forest-glades, I entreat you ! Dorian waters, cry
For Bion the dear and sweet ! Wail, rivers, in sympathy !
All green things, mourn, I pray you ! Moan, ye wood-lawns, now !
Flowers, breathe your life away, let your faded clusters bow !
O roses, for grief blush ye, O windflower, flush thou red !
Speak, bluebell, thy letters of woe ; let a darker ' AI, AI ' show
In thy sad embroidery ! The beautiful poet is dead !
  O Muses Sicilian, awake the dirge for Bion's sake !
O nightingales, ye which knell amid leaves thick-clustering
Your wail, to the waters tell it of Arethusa's spring   10

That Bion the herdman hath died, that with him hath passed away
All song from the country-side, that dead is the Dorian lay.
   O Muses Sicilian, awake the dirge for Bion's sake!
Swans, waken the dolorous note where Strymon's waters flow ;
Pour from a wailing throat the music of all your woe—
Such a song as himself once sang, which he learnt from your mouths as
     it rang :—
To the Muses Oeagrian cry, and to all the Nymphs be it said,
Wood-queens of Bistony, that the Orpheus of Doris is dead.
   O Muses Sicilian, awake the dirge for Bion's sake!
He, the belovèd one of his kine, will sing not again :   20
Never more 'neath the oak-trees lone will he sit and chant the strain ;
But in Pluto's presence he sings oblivion of earthly things.
Voiceless the mountains stand : the kine, by the bulls as they stray,
Moan through the sighing land, and they turn from the pasture away.
   O Muses Sicilian, awake the dirge for Bion's sake!
O Bion, Apollo condoled with thy swift doom, shedding the tear :
Mourned Satyrs, and sable-stoled the Priapuses wept on thy bier.
For thy lost song Wood-gods groan ; through the forest the Well-maids
     yearned
For thee, and with tears made moan, and their tears into rivulets turned.
Echo is mourning sore mid her rocks, for that hushed is thy breath,   30
And she mimics thy lips no more. The trees because of thy death
Have cast their fruit, and strowed are the faded flowers on the ground.
No milk from the ewes hath flowed, in the hives no honey is found ;
For the grief of the bees maketh dearth in the comb : no man cares now,
When thine honey hath perished from earth, to gather their honey, I
     trow !
   O Muses Sicilian, awake the dirge for Bion's sake!
Never hath Siren so lamented by crag-hung shore ;
Never such note of woe mid the rocks did the nightingale pour ;
Never so piercingly wailed the swallow on hill-ridges long ;
Never halcyon so hath scaled the heavens with dolorous song ;   40
Never sea-mew's plaint was so wild where the grey waves sighing fell,
Nor so shrilly for Memnon, child of the Dawn, in the Dawn-queen's dell

Shrieked the Memnonian bird, around his sepulchre flying,
As now were their voices heard all wailing for Bion's dying.
  O Muses Sicilian, awake the dirge for Bion's sake!
Nightingales, swallows, each and all, whom he gladdened so
Once, when he taught them our speech, sat and wailed on the branches
    arow
In antiphons dolorous : all birds took up the refrain—
" Wail on, ye mourners, with us : we sorrow too in your pain ! "
  O Muses Sicilian, awake the dirge for Bion's sake!   50
Who now on thy pipe shall play, O minstrel thrice-desired ?
Who to thy reeds shall lay his lips, presumption-fired ?
For yet with thy lips do they thrill, thy breath there lingereth long :
And amidst of her reed-beds still feeds Echo upon thy song.
This pipe unto Pan shall I bear ? Nay, he haply might fear, even he,
To press his divine lips there, lest we crown him but second to thee !
  O Muses Sicilian, awake the dirge for Bion's sake!
For thy song Galatea doth weep, whom thou didst gladden of yore
When, overlooking the deep, she sat by thy side on the shore.
Not as thine was the minstrelsy of the Cyclops : shrank from his
    face   60
That fair one ; more sweetly on thee than on salt sea-waves did she
    gaze.
And now she remembers no more the joy of the heaving brine,
But she sits by the lone sea-shore, and she tends thy masterless kine.
  O Muses Sicilian, awake the dirge for Bion's sake!
All gifts that the Song-queens brought, O herdman, with thee have
    perished :
Girls' love-thrilling kisses are naught, and the lips of the child heart-
    cherished.
Eroses weep on thy tomb, from their faces hath faded the bloom.
Dear art thou to Cypris above that last long kiss that lay
On the lips of Adonis her love, when his life was fleeting away.
  O Muses Sicilian, awake the dirge for Bion's sake!   70
Lo, Meles, most musical of rivers, thy second woe !
On thee doth a new pang fall. Thine Homer was lost long ago—

Sweet mouth of the Queen of Song !—and thou, as the old tales run,
With floods of weeping long didst mourn for thy noble son,
And all the briny deep did thy crying fill.   Now again
For another son dost thou weep, and dost pine with a new heart-
  pain.
Of Fountains beloved were the twain : of Pegasus' well one quaffed :
The other was wont to drain Arethusa's magic draught.
This lifted his voice to sing of Helen's beauty divine,
And of Thetis' great son, and of King Menelaus of Atreus' line ;   80
That sang not of wars nor of weeping ; of Pan his woodnotes rang,
And of herdmen he piped, and keeping the pasturing kine he sang.
He fashioned the pipe of the reed, he milked his kine in the mead,
Love-lore he taught to the young, and he drew love close to his heart,
And he sang how Adonis stung Aphrodite with passion's dart.
  O Muses Sicilian, awake the dirge for Bion's sake !
Each world-famed burg wails o'er thee, Bion, and every town :
Yea, Accra laments thee more than her Hesiod, who gave her renown :
Not forests Boeotian yearn so sorely for Pindar's return,
Nor so wept Lesbos for pity when passed Alcaeus away,   90
Nor so did the Teian city bewail her bard's lost lay.
Thee gladlier Paros would see than Archilochus : now no more
Mytilene for Sappho, but thee, doth in music her sorrow outpour.
All herdmen of voice high-soaring in song, who have heard the call
Of the Muses, thy doom are deploring ; they weep for thy death one and
  all.
Sicelidas, Samos' glory, is weeping : Cydonia's child,
Lycidas, sheddeth tears for thy story—he from whose eyes, as they
  smiled,
A splendour of gladness broke.   And Philetas outwaileth his woe
Amidst the Triopian folk, where Hales' waters flow.
And Theocritus sings sorrow's strain in Syracuse : I chant now   100
The dirge of Ausonia's pain : no stranger am I, I trow,
Unto Pastoral Song.   I am heir of the Dorian Muse, which was taught
Unto thy disciples by thee ; yea, this was thy gift unto me.
Others thy wealth may share, but thy mantle of song I caught.

O Muses Sicilian, awake the dirge for Bion's sake!
Alas and alas ! when dead in the garden the mallow lies,
Or the parsley's greenness is fled, or the anise's lush wreath dies,
When a few short months are sped, to a new year's life will they rise :
But we men, great and strong, the wisdom of ages who reap,
When this one life hath flown, into hollows of earth are thrown,   110
And slumber there through the long, long hush of the morningless sleep.
And thou in the earth shalt abide, thee veils of silence shall hide.
Yet did the Muses ordain that the *frog* should unendingly sing !
I envy him not, for his strain is an all-unlovely thing.
O Muses Sicilian, awake the dirge for Bion's sake!
To thy lips came poisoned wine, O Bion, thy death they quaffed.
Not even such lips as thine could sweeten the bitter draught.
What mortal so heartless of soul could mingle the venom for thee,
Or give such singer the bowl ?—a hater of song was he !
O Muses Sicilian, awake the dirge for Bion's sake!   120
But justice hath reached them all.   Yet I mourn for thy darkened light,
And the tears of my sorrow fall evermore.   But oh, if I might,
Like Orpheus, to Hades go down, as Odysseus of yore descended,
And Alcides of older renown, so I to the mansion had wended
Of Pluto, to gaze upon thee, and, if thou unto him singest now,
To hearken thy minstrelsy :—now nay, unto Cora do thou
On the strings Sicilian play, sing some sweet pastoral lay !
Of Sicily is she too ; she sported in Etna's glens,
And the Dorian strain she knew : the song whose notes ring thence
Shall be surely rewarded.   She granted to Orpheus a boon of yore,   130
To his harp when sweetly he chanted : Eurydice did she restore.
Thee too will she send to thine hills.   Ah, could my piping have wrung
Aught from those iron wills, before Pluto had I too sung.

IDYLL IV.

The lure of the sea and the charm of the land.

WHEN softly the wind is kissing the face of the grey salt sea,
Mine heavy heart is requickened : no longer lovely to me
Is the land ; far more am I drawn by his lure of tranquillity.
But when his abysses are hoary and crying aloud, and the wave
Topples white-crested with foam, and the long-backed surges rave,
To the land and its trees do I turn mine eyes, and I flee from the flood ;
The lea stretcheth welcoming arms, and the shady trees of the wood ;
And there, when the great blasts blow, the pine-tree sings to me " Come ! "
O, the fisherman's life is a joyless life, whose boat is his home,
And the sea is the field he must plough, and the fish his elusive prey.   10
But for me sweet sleep 'neath the plane's dense leaves that dreamily sway !
To the sound of the fountain falling anear let me hearken with joy,
As it whispers delight to the toiler, and hath not a note of annoy.

IDYLL V.

Love's cross-purposes.

IN love with Echo his neighbour was Pan ; Echo's whole heart turned
To the fawn-footed Satyr ; the Satyr for Lyde in frenzy burned.
As Echo inflamed Pan's heart, the Satyr set Echo's aflame,
And Lyde the Satyr's : the torture of love was for each the same.
So in measure as each of these did despite to a loving heart,
With hate was their own love met ; each suffered scorned love's smart.
To all earth's loveless ones I therefore proclaim this warning :
" Love them that love you, and so shall your love win love, not scorning."

IDYLL VI.

The River-god who loved the Fountain-nymph.

WHEN Alpheius, from Pisa departing, journeyeth under the sea,
He brings Arethusa the waters that nurture the olive-tree,
Bears bridal-gifts, fair leaves and flowers and sacred soil.
Deep under the billows he plunges : far under the sea like oil
He races, for never mingle his streams with the waters' flow :
Of the river that rusheth through her nothing the sea doth know.
That knavish Boy, that teacher of naughtiness, mischief-contriver,
Love, by his spells made even a river a deep-sea-diver !

IDYLL VII.

Eros at the plough.

HE laid down torch and bow, a goad he took in his hand—
  Mischievous Love—a wallet upon his back he bare.
He bowed the neck of a toil-strong bull 'neath the broad yoke-band :
  He strode o'er Demeter's furrows, he sowed the wheat-grains there.
He looked up to the sky unto Zeus, he cried : " Ho, water my land,
  Lest I take thee, O Bull of Europa, and make thee drag the share ! "

IDYLL VIII.

Heart's ease in song.

OH that my father had taught me to pasture the thick-fleeced sheep !
Then a seat 'neath the elms had I sought, or 'neath rocks looking over the
    deep,
Piping a strain that my love's long pain in oblivion should steep.

For EU product safety concerns, contact us at Calle de José Abascal, 56–1°, 28003 Madrid, Spain or eugpsr@cambridge.org.

www.ingramcontent.com/pod-product-compliance
Ingram Content Group UK Ltd.
Pitfield, Milton Keynes, MK11 3LW, UK
UKHW030902150625
459647UK00021B/2670